Rosicrucian Trio

The Rosicrucian Manifestos

*Fama Fraternitatis, Confessio Fraternitatis and
Chymical Wedding of Christian Rosenkreutz*

Introduction by
Michael R. Poll

A Cornerstone Book

Rosicrucian Trio
The Rosicrucian Manifestos
Introduction by Michael R. Poll

A Cornerstone Book
Published by Cornerstone Book Publishers
An imprint of Michael Poll Publishing
Copyright © 2019 by Cornerstone Book Publishers

Cornerstone Book Publishers
Hot Springs Village, AR
Cornerstone Edition - 2019
www.cornerstonepublishers.com

Table of Contents

EMBLEMA I
AURI POTABILIS CHIMICE
PRÆPARATI

Introduction

The first time that I read the *Rosicrucian Manifestos* I was in my late teens or early twenties. I was not exactly sure what I was reading. They were so... odd. But, I kept coming back to them. Over the years, my opinion of these manifestos changed with nearly every reading. Were they nonsense, an actual blueprint to turn base metal into gold, or something else? Today, I see them as something *more*. I believe them to be layered symbolic code designed to be a notice or "calling out" to those who may be kindred spirits. The message is simple: "We can help you become more than you are today." The idea that these individuals were either crazy or involved simply in a highly complex and creative plan to gain monetary wealth is, to me, an affront to any discerning person. But, why in the world were these manifestos written in such a strange and confusingly complex manner?

If the *Rosicrucian Manifestos* were designed to bring attention to a small, select grouping of seekers with the desire of improving their lives, then why did they go to such great lengths to cleverly encode the meaning of these manifestos? Why couldn't they just say who they were and what they were offering? I believe that we must remember the times in which these manifestos were written. These manifestos were written and published in Germany in the early 1600's. Europe was just coming out of the Dark Ages. The times were very difficult, dangerous, and restrictive. People were put to death for merely translating the Bible. Education was controlled and even illegal if it did not mimic the teachings, and received the blessings of the Church. So, what could be done if someone held opinions that differed from the Church? What if they had questions that the Church did not want asked or answered? What if a sincere student wanted to explore ideas and concepts that were outside of what the Church allowed? What could be done? With this mindset, the manner in which the *Manifestos* were written does start to make sense.

In looking back at human history, early humans faced a harsh and unforgiving existence. Their intellectual development had not yet been fully developed yet were driven with all their being to grow and become more than what they were. Fear often kept them alive. But, they overcame fear time and again if it meant the opportunity to grow. Can you imagine the terror they must have felt when they were huddled together in small caves during thunderstorms? What was it? What caused it? Who or what was behind what seemed to be an attack on them? They understood that it was something loud and dangerous, but they did not understand its nature. It was beyond everything that they could control or fight. And then the ground shook with tremendous explosions of thunder. They could see lightening hitting trees near them. Can you imagine how they felt? Did a god enter the trees? Yet, with terror in their hearts, they *had* to go out and touch the trees hit by the lightening. They *had* to do it. They could not stop themselves from the overpowering desire to try to understand — to learn and grow. And, humanity did grow, learn and prosper. Great civilizations were created. When they died, new ones took their place. The progress of humanity was clearly upwards — until the Dark Ages.

Western Civilization was devastated by the Dark Ages. All social, educational, and cultural progress halted. Those who held power realized that an ignorant population was far easier to control than an educated one. The general population became an ignorant society. Standards of living and all aspects of the once great Western Civilization declined rapidly. The great mistake, however, was in the belief that you can forever hold humanity down and stop its growth.

For the most part, the Church controlled what people believed. The control of the population was accomplished by fear. For some, the effective threat was fear of eternal, fiery damnation promised to any who challenged or violated the Church's teachings. An eternity of unspeakable pain and suffering was enough for most to stay far within the dogma of the Church. But, for those who openly spoke out, or challenged the Church's authority, the pain and suffering was turned into reality. Many were subjected to horrifying deaths at the hands of the Church. The threats were not empty.

But from the beginning of the Dark Ages, there were some who continued to think, question, and wonder. After a time, these brave spirits began to secretly gather in small groups to share dangerous thoughts and questions. Forbidden subjects such as science, astronomy, medicine, and religion were just some of the subjects discussed and studied. They were *growing* at these meetings, and it was an unquenchable thirst to grow. They all knew the penalty if their activity was discovered, so great care was made to keep private the meetings and those attending. Vows of secrecy were taken, and complex codes and protection were created. The little groups wanted to continue meeting — they *needed* to continue meeting — so, they did what they felt was necessary to protect themselves and the work that they were doing.

If you think about what the members of these little groups were doing and how they operated, an interesting picture starts to develop. They wanted — *needed* — to discuss and explore forbidden subjects with the full knowledge that what they were doing was punishable by imprisonment or death. They were doing nothing evil or immoral (these subjects are today taught in public schools), but they knew that if they did not take precautions, they could suffer greatly, and the work would cease. It was necessary to continue the work while protecting the members from actual danger. What they were doing is very similar to early man going out and touching the tree hit by lightening. They knew that what they were doing could possibly be very harmful, and they may have had great fear in their hearts, but they *had* to do it. They had to know. They had to understand. The quest for knowledge was hard-wired into them.

The little groups had a finite number of members. With time, everyone lives and dies. If the work was to continue, new members would be needed. But, how do you recruit members to do very important secret work that could result in their death if discovered? Ingenious and misleading covers were created to throw unfriendly eyes off the path of the members of the little groups. Rather than allowing themselves to be seen as researchers seeking the meaning of life and how to best live it, they portrayed themselves as nutty old charlatans in search of easy gold. Their covers were strange and touched on greed (understood by all). How these alchemists could actually create gold from base metals was not at all understood by anyone. But, they all did, very clearly, understand that *if* this could be done, then maybe *they* could gain riches from what these crazy old men were doing. Maybe it was best to be friendly to them and leave them alone. Many times that is exactly what happened. If what they were doing was of value, then they might all benefit (especially royalty). If what they were doing was a waste, then the alchemists were all mad and not worth time or attention.

Make no mistake, these "nutty old men" were brilliant scientists. Yes, they were able to make gold — or something that could not, at that time, be distinguished from gold. Today, "fake gold" is a danger to all pawn shops or jewelers who buy gold or gold jewelry. What looks, feels and to most all common tests, is gold can be created in labs (or, someone's basement). It's not impossible nonsense. In some cases, it takes sophisticated modern equipment to tell the man-made gold from the real. The same is true of precious gems. They can be "grown" in large batches at a fraction of the cost of real precious gems. This simulated gold and gems are often used in the creation of new pieces of jewelry. By using imitation material, if something is damaged or ruined in the creation process, the loss is not as serious as if real gold or gems were used.

The little groups of old knew that most people would not be suitable or interested in their real work. The manifestos were not for them. The groups also knew that care had to be taken with trying to gather new members as their real work was outlawed. Their secret could not be discovered. Anything that was published ran the risk of discovery and serious consequences. *The Rosicrucian Manifestos* were written and published in a manner that seemed to be almost meaningless babble to those with no interest in it or those with a desire to punish *seekers of Light*. But, for the few who could read between the lines and see the "real gold," these membership advertisements, or calls, were successful.

The Rosicrucian Trio (Rosicrucian Manifestos) were published anonymously. But, from early days they have been attributed to Johann Valentin Andreae, Francis Bacon, and others. Clearly someone, or more than one, set the words to paper. For me, however, the original author is nowhere near as important as the message or the story within the story. We are not so advanced today that we don't need the help that the little hidden groups provided. Big titles, impressive sounding offices, and massive egos are the "gold" of the old alchemists. It is the nonsense that we must wade through to find what is of real value. We do need this now as much as ever.

Michael R. Poll
December, 2019

Rosicrucian Trio
The Rosicrucian Manifestos

IGNIS.

AERIS.

AQVÆ.

TERRÆ.

TINCTVR.
COAGVLATION.
DISTILLATION.
PVTREFACTION.
SOLVTION.
SVBLIMATION.
CALTINATION.

Fama Fraternitatis

Anonymous, 1614
the first Rosicrucian Manifesto

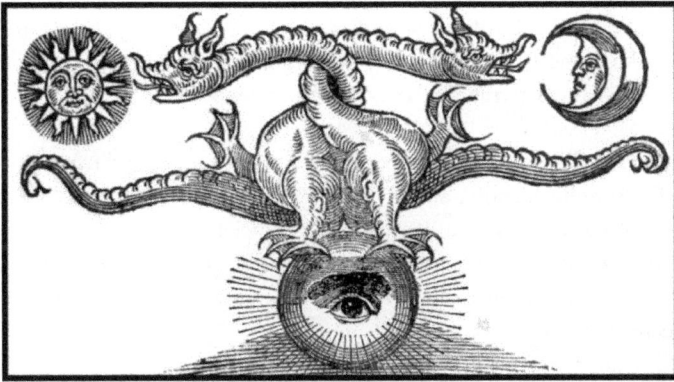

To the Wise and Understanding Reader.

Wisdom (said Solomon) is to a man an infinite Treasure, for she is the Breath of the Power of God, and a pure Influence that flowers from the Glory of the Almighty; she is the Brightness of Eternal Light, and an undefiled Mirror of the Majesty of God, and an Image of his Goodness; she teaches us Soberness and Prudence, Righteousness and Strength; she understands the Subtlety of words, and Solution of dark sentences; she foreknows Signs and Wonders, and what shall happen in time to come; with this Treasure was our first Father Adam fully endued: Hence it doth appear, that after God had brought before him all the Creatures of the Field, and the Fowls under Heaven, he gave to every one of them their proper names, according to their nature.

Although now through the sorrowful fall into sin this excellent Jewel Wisdom had been lost, and Darkness and Ignorance is come into the World, yet notwithstanding had the Lord God sometimes hitherto bestowed, and made manifest the same, to some of his Friends: For the wise King Solomon doth testify of himself, that he upon earnest prayer and desire did get and obtain such Wisdom of God, that thereby he knew how the World was created, thereby he understood the Nature of the Elements, also the time, beginning, middle and end, the increase and decrease,

1

the change of times through the whole Year, the Revolution of the Year, and Ordinance of the Stars; he understood also the properties of tame and wild Beasts, the cause of the raging of the Winds, and minds and intents of men, all sorts and natures of Plants, virtues of Roots, and others, was not unknown to him. Now I do not think that there can be found anyone who would not wish and desire with all his heart to be a Partaker of this noble Treasure; but seeing the same Felicity can happen to none, except God himself give Wisdom, and send his holy Spirit from above, we have therefore set forth in print this little Treatise, to wit, *Famam & Confessionem,* of the Laudable Fraternity of the Rosie Cross, to be read by everyone, because in them is clearly shown and discovered, what concerning it the World had to expect.

Although these things may seem somewhat strange, and many may esteem it to be but a Philosophical show, and no true History, which is published and spoken of the Fraternity of the Rosie Cross; it shall here sufficiently appear by our Confession, that there is more than may be imagined; and it shall be easily understood, and observed by everyone (if he be not altogether void of understanding) what today, and at these times, is meant thereby.

Those who are true Disciples of Wisdom, and true Followers of the Spherical Art, will consider better of these things, and have them in greater estimation, as also judge far otherwise of them, as had been done by some principal Persons, but especially of Adam Haselmeyer, *Notarius Publicus* to the Arch Duke Maximilian, who likewise had made an *Extract ex scriptis Theologicis Theophrasti*, and written a Treatise under the Title of *Jesuiter*, wherein he desires, that every Christian should be a true Jesuit, that is, to walk, live, be, and remain in Jesus: He was but ill rewarded of the Jesuits, because in his answer written upon the *Famam*, he did name those of the *Fraternity of the Rosie Cross*, The highly illuminated men, and undeceiving Jesuits; for they not able to brook this, laid hands on him, and put him into the *Galleis*, for which they likewise have to expect their reward.

Blessed Aurora will now henceforth begin to appear, who (after the passing away of the dark Night of Saturn) with her Brightness altogether extinguishing the shining of the Moon, or the small Sparks of Heavenly Wisdom, which yet remains with men, and is a Forerunner of pleasant Phebus, who with his clear and fiery glistering Beams brings forth that blessed Day, long wished for, of many truehearted; by which Daylight then shall truly be known, and shall be seen all heavenly Treasures of godly Wisdom, as also the Secrets of all hidden and invisible things in the World, according to the Doctrine of our Forefathers, and ancient Wise men.

This will be the right kingly Ruby, and most excellent shining Carbuncle, of the which it is said, That he doth shine and give light in darkness, and to be a perfect

Medicine of all imperfect Bodies, and to change them into the best Gold, and to cure all Diseases of Men, easing them of all pains and miseries.

Be therefore, gentle Reader, admonished, that with me you do earnestly pray to God, that it please him to open the hearts and ears of all ill hearing people, and to grant unto them his blessing, that they may be able to know him in his Omni-potency, with admiring contemplation of Nature, to his honor and praise, and to the love, help, comfort and strengthening of our Neighbors, and to the restoring of all the diseased.

Fama Fraternitatis, or, A Discovery
of the Fraternity of the most laudable
Order of the Rosy Cross.

Seeing the only Wise and Merciful God in these latter days had poured out so richly his mercy and goodness to Mankind, whereby we do attain more and more to the perfect knowledge of his Son Jesus Christ and Nature, that justly we may boast of the happy time, wherein there is not only discovered unto us the half part of the World, which was heretofore unknown & hidden, but he had also made manifest unto us many wonderful, and never-heretofore see, Works and Creatures of Nature, and moreover had raised men, endued with great Wisdom, which might partly renew and reduce all Arts (in this our Age spotted and imperfect) to perfection; so that finally Man might thereby understand his own Nobleness and Worth, and why he is called *Microcosmus*, and how far his knowledge extends in Nature.

Although the rude World herewith will be but little pleased, but rather smile and scoff thereat; also the Pride and Covetousness of the Learned is so great, it will not suffer them to agree together; but were they united, they might out of all those things which in this our Age God doth so richly bestow upon us, collect *Librum Naturae*, or a perfect Method of all Arts: but such is their opposition, that they still keep, and are loath to leave the old course, esteeming Porphiry, Aristotle, and Galen, and that which had but a bit of learning, more than the clear and manifested Light and Truth; who if they were now living, with much joy would leave their erroneous Doctrines. But here are too great weaknesses for such a great Work: And although in Theology, Physic, and the Mathematic, the Truth doth oppose itself; nevertheless, the old Enemy by his subtlety and craft does show himself in hindering every good purpose by his Instruments and con-tentious wavering people. To such an intent of a general Reformation, the most godly and highly illuminated Father, our Brother, C.R. a German, the chief and original of our Fraternity, had much and long time labored, who by reason of his poverty (although descended of Noble Parents) in the fifth year of his age was placed in a Cloyster, where he had learned indifferently the Greek and Latin Tongues, who (upon his earnest desire and request) being yet in his growing years, was associated to a Brother, P.A.L. who had determined to go to the Holy Land.

Although this Brother died in Cyprus, and so never came to Jerusalem, yet our Brother C.R. did not return, but shipped himself over, and went to Damascus, minding from thence to go to Jerusalem; but by reason of the feebleness of his body he remained still there, and by his skill in Physics he obtained much favor with the Turks. In the mean time he became by chance acquainted with the Wise men of Damascus in Arabia, and beheld what great Wonders they wrought, and how Nature was discovered unto them; hereby was that high and noble Spirit of Brother C.R. so stirred up, that Jerusalem was not so much now in his mind as Damasco; also he could not bridle his desires any longer, but made a bargain with the Arabians, that they should carry him for a certain sum of money to Damascus; he was only of the age of sixteen years when he came thither, yet of a strong Dutch constitution; there the Wise received him (as he himself witnessed) not as a stranger, but as one whom they had long expected, they called him by his name, and showed him other secrets out of his Cloyster, whereat he could not but mightily wonder: He learned there better the Arabian Tongue; so that the year following he translated the *Book M* into good Latin, which he afterwards brought with him. This is the place where he did learn his Physics, and his Mathematics, whereof the World had just cause to rejoice, if there were more Love, and less Envy. After three years he returned again with good consent, shipped himself over Sinus Arabicus into Egypt, where he remained not long, but only took better notice there of the Plants and Creatures; he sailed over the whole Mediterranean Sea for to come unto Fez, where the Arabians had directed him. And it is a great shame unto us, that wise men, so far remote the one from the other, should not only be of one opinion, hating all contentious Writings, but also be so willing and ready under the seal of secrecy to impart their secrets to others.

Every year the Arabians and Africans do send one to another, inquiring one of another out of their Arts, if happily they had found out some better things, or if Experience had weakened their Reasons. Yearly there came something to light, whereby the Mathematics, Physics and Magic (for in those are they of Fez most skillful) were amended; as there is nowadays in Germany no want of learned Men, Magicians, Cabalists, Physicians, and Philosophers, were there but more love and kindness among them, or that the most part of them would not keep their secrets close only to themselves. At Fez he did get acquaintance with those which are commonly called the Elementary Inhabitants, who revealed unto him many of their secrets: As we Germans likewise might gather together many things, if there were the like unity, and desire of searching out of secrets amongst us.

Of these of Fez he often did confess, that their Magic was not altogether pure, and also that their Cabala was defiled with their Religion; but notwithstanding he

4

knew how to make good use of the same, and found still more better grounds of his Faith, altogether agreeable with the Harmony of the whole World, and wonderfully impressed in all Periods of times, and then proceeding that fair Concord, that as in every several kernel is contained a whole good tree or fruit, so likewise is included in the little body of Man the whole great World, whose Religion, policy, health, members, nature, language, words and works, are agreeing, sympathizing, and in equal tune and melody with God, Heaven and Earth; and that which is disagreeing with them, is error, falsehood and of the Devil, who alone is the first, middle, and last cause of strife, blindness, and darkness in the World: Also, might one examine all and several persons upon the Earth, he should find that which is good and right, is always agreeing with itself; but all the rest is spotted with a thousand erroneous conceits.

After two years Brother R.C. departed the City Fez, and sailed with many costly things into Spain, hoping, he himself had so well and so profitably spent his time in his travel, that the learned in Europe would highly rejoice with him, and begin to rule, and order all their Studies, according to those sound and sure Foundations. He therefore conferred with the Learned in Spain, showing unto them the Errors of our Arts, and how they might be corrected, and from whence they should gather the true *Inditia* of the Times to come, and wherein they ought to agree with those things that are past; also how the faults of the Church and the whole *Philosopia Moralis* was to be amended. He showed them new Growths, new Fruits, and Beasts, which did concord with old Philosophy, and prescribed them new *Axiomata*, whereby all things might fully be restored. But it was to them a laughing matter; and being a new thing unto them, they feared that their great Name should be lessened, if they should now again begin to learn and acknowledge their many years of Errors, to which they were accustomed, and wherewith they had gained them enough. Who so loved chaos let him be reformed.

The same Song was also sang to him by other Nations, the which moved him the more (because it happened to him contrary to his expectation,) being then ready bountifully to impart all his Arts and Secrets to the Learned, if they would have but undertaken to write the true and infallible *Axiomata*, out of all Faculties, Sciences and Arts, and whole Nature, as that which he knew would direct them, like a Globe, or Circle, to the middle Point, and Centrum, and (as it is usual among the Arabians) it should serve to the wise and learned for a Rule, that also there might be a Society in Europe, which might have Gold, Silver, and precious Stones, sufficient for to bestow them on Kings, for their necessary uses, and lawful purposes: with which such as be Governors might be brought up, for to learn all that which God had suffered Man to know, and thereby to be enabled in all times of need to give their counsel unto those that seek it, like the *Heathen Oracles:* Verily we must confess that the world in those days was already big with those great Commotions, laboring to be delivered of them; and did bring forth painful, worthy men, who brake with all force through Darkness and Barbarism, and left us who succeeded to follow them: and assuredly they have been the uppermost point in *Trygono igneo,* whose flame now should be more and more brighter, and shall undoubtedly give to the World the last Light.

Such a one likewise had Theophrastus been in Vocation and Callings, although he was none of our Fraternity, yet nevertheless had he diligently read over the Book M: whereby his sharp ingenious was exalted; but this man was also hindered in his course by the multitude of the learned and wise-seeming men, that he was never able peaceably to confer with others of his Knowledge and Understanding he had of Nature. And therefore in his writing he rather mocked these busy bodies, and does not show them altogether what he was: yet nevertheless there is found with him well grounded the aforenamed Harmonia, which without doubt he had imparted to the Learned, if he had not found them rather worthy of subtle vexation, then to be instructed in greater Arts and Sciences; he then with a free and careless life lost his time, and left unto the World their foolish pleasures.

But that we do not forget our loving Father, Brother C.R. he after many painful Travels, and his fruitless true Instructions, returned again into Germany, the which he (by reason of the alterations which were shortly to come, and of the strange and dangerous contentions) heartily loved. There, although he could have bragged with his Art, but specially of the transmutations of Metals; yet did he esteem more Heaven, and the Citizens thereof, Man, then all vain glory and pomp.

Nevertheless, he built a fitting and neat inhabitation, in the which he ruminated his Voyage, and Philosophy, and reduced them together in a true Memorial. In this house he spent a great time in the Mathematics, and made many fine Instruments, *ex omnibus hujus artis partibus,* whereof there is but little remaining to us, as hereafter you shall understand. After five years came again into his mind the wished for Reformation; and in regard he doubted of the aid and help of others, although he himself was painful, lusty, and hardy, he undertook, with some few adjoined with him, to attempt the same: wherefore he desired to that end, to have out of his first Cloister (to the which he bare a great affection) three of his Brethren, Brother G.V. Brother J.A. and Brother J.O. who besides that, they had some more knowledge in the Arts, then at that time many others had, he did bind those three unto himself, to be faithful, diligent, and secret; as also to commit carefully to writing, all that which he should direct and instruct them in, to the end that those which were to come, and through especial Revelation should be received into this Fraternity, might not be deceived of the least syllable and word.

After this manner began the Fraternity of the Rosie Cross; first, by four persons , and by them was made the Magical Language and writing, with a large

6

Dictionary, which we yet daily use to God's praise and glory, and do find great wisdom therein; they made also the first part of the *Book M*: but in respect that the labor was too heavy, and the unspeakable concourse of the sick hindered them, and also whilst his new building (called *Sancti spiritus*) was now finished, they concluded to draw and receive yet others more into their Fraternity; to this end was chosen brother R.C. his deceased fathers brothers son, brother B. a skilful Painter, G. and P.D. their Secretary, all Germans except J.A. so in all they were eight in number, all bachelors and of vowed virginity, by those was collected a book or volume of all that which man can desire, wish, or hope for.

Although we do now freely confess, that the World is much amended within an hundred years, yet we are assured, that our *Axiomata* shall immovably remain unto the Worlds End, and also the world in her highest and last Age shall not attain to see anything else; for our Rota takes her beginning from that day when God spoke *Fiat*, and shall end when he shall speak Pereat; yet Gods Clock strikes every minute, where ours scarce strikes perfect hours. We also steadfastly believe, that if our Brethren and Fathers had lived in this our present and clear light, they would more roughly have handled the Pope, Mahomet, Scribes, Artists, and Sophisters, and had showed themselves more helpful, not simply with sighs, and wishing of their end and consummation.

When now these eight Brethren had disposed and ordered all things in such manner, as there was not now need of any great labor, and also that everyone was sufficiently instructed, and able perfectly to discourse of secret and manifest Philosophy, they would not remain any longer together, but as in the beginning they had agreed, they separated themselves into several Countries, because that not only their Axiomata might in secret be more profoundly examined by the learned, but that they themselves, if in some Country or other they observed anything, or perceived some Error, they might inform one another of it.

Their agreement was this:

1. *That none of them should profess any other thing, then to   cure the sick, and that gratis.*
2. *None of the Posterity should be constrained to wear one certain kind of habit, but therein to follow the custom of the Country.*
3. *That every year upon the day C. they should meet at the house S.Spiritus, or to write the cause of his absence.*
4. *Every Brother should look out for a worthy person, who after his death might succeed him.*
5. *The word C.R. should be their Seal, Mark, and Character.*
6. *The Fraternity should remain secret one hundred years.*

These six Articles they bound themselves one to another to keep; and five of the Brethren departed, only the Brethren B. and D. remained with the Father Fra: R.C. a whole year; when these likewise departed, then remained by him his Cousin and Brother J.O. so that he had all the days of his life with him two of his Brethren. And although that as yet the Church was not cleansed, nevertheless we know that they did think of her, and with what longing desire they looked for: Every year they assembled together with joy, and made a full resolution of that which they had done; there must certainly have been great pleasure, to hear truly and without invention related and rehearsed all the Wonders which God had poured out here and there through the World. Every one may hold it out for certain, that such persons as were sent, and joined together by God, and the Heavens, and chosen out of the wisest of men, as have lived in many Ages, did live together above all others in highest Unity, greatest Secrecy, and most kindness one towards another.

After such a most laudable sort they did spend their lives; and although they were free from all diseases and pain, yet notwithstanding they could not live and pass their time appointed of God. The first of this Fraternity which died, and that in England, was J.O. as Brother C. long before had foretold him; he was very expert, and well learned in Cabala, as his Book called H. witnessed. In England he is much spoken of, and chiefly because he cured a young Earl of Norfolk of the Leprosie. They had concluded, that as much as possibly could be their burial place should be kept secret, as at this day it is not known unto us what is become of some of them, yet every ones place was supplied with a fit successor; but this we will confess publicly by these presents to the honor of God, That what secret so ever we have learned out of the *Book M.* (although before our eyes we behold the image and pattern of all the world) yet are there not shown unto us our misfortunes, nor hour of death, the which only is known to God himself, who thereby would have us keep in a continual readiness; but hereof more in our Confession, where we do set down 37 Reasons wherefore we now do make known our Fraternity, and proffer such high Mysteries freely, and without constraint and reward: also we do promise more gold then both the Indies bring to the King of Spain; for Europe is with child and will bring forth a strong child, who shall stand in need of a great godfathers gift.

After the death of I.O. Brother R.C. rested not, but as soon as he could, called the rest together, (and as we suppose) then his grave was made; although hitherto we (who were the latest) did not know when our loving father R.C. died, and had no more but the bare names of the beginners, and all their successors to us; yet there came into our memory, a secret, which through dark and hidden words, and speeches of the 100 years, brother A. the successor of D. (who was of the last and second row and succession), and had lived amongst many of us,) did impart unto us of the third row and succession; otherwise we must confess, that after the death of the said A. none of us had in any manner known anything of Brother R.C. and of his first fellow brethren, then that which was extant of them in our *Philosophical Bibliotheca,* amongst which our *Axiomata* was held for the chief *Rota Mundi*, for the most artificial, and *Protheus* the most profitable. Likewise we do not certainly know if these of the second row have been of the like wisdom as the first, and if they were admitted to all things. It shall be declared hereafter to the gentle Reader, not what we have heard of the burial of R.C. but also made manifest publicly by the foresight, sufferance and commandment of God, whom we most faithfully obey, that if we shall be answered discreetly and Christian-like, we will not be afraid to set forth publicly in Print, our names, and sir names, our meetings, or anything else that may be required at our hands.

Now the true and fundamental relation of the finding out of the high illuminated man of God, Fra: C.R.C. is this; After that A. in *Gallia Narbonensi* was deceased, then seceded in his place, our loving Brother N.N. this man after he had repaired unto us to take the solemn oath of fidelity and secrecy, he informed us bona fide, that A. had comforted him in telling him, that this Fraternity should ere long not remain so hidden, but should be to all the whole German Nation helpful, needful, and commendable; of the which he was not in any wise in his estate ashamed of. The year following after he had performed his School right, and was minded now to travel, being for that purpose sufficiently provided with Fortunate purse, he thought (he being a good Architect) to alter something of his building, and to make it more fit: in such renewing he lighted upon the memorial Table which was cast of brass, and contains all the names of the brethren, with some few other things; this he would transfer in another more fitting vault: for where or when Fra: R.C. died, or in what country he was buried, was by our predecessors concealed and unknown unto us. In this Table stuck a great nail somewhat strong, so that when he was with force drawn out, he took with him an indifferent large stone out of the thin wall, or plastering of the hidden door, and so unlooked for uncovered the door; wherefore we did with joy and longing throw down the rest of the wall, and cleared the door, upon which that was written in great letters, Post 120 *annos patebo,* with the year of the Lord under it: therefore we gave God thanks and let it rest that same night, because first we would overlook our *Rotam*; but we refer our selves again to the confession, for what we here publish is done for the help of those that are worthy, but to the unworthy (God willing) it will be small profit: For like as our door was after so many years wonderfully discovered, also there shall be opened a door to Europe (when the wall is removed) which already does begin to appear, and with great desire is expected of many.

In the morning following we opened the door, and there appeared to our sight a Vault of seven sides and corners, every side five for broad, and the height of eight foot; Although the Sun never shined in this Vault, nevertheless it was enlightened with another sun, which had learned this from the Sun, and was situated in the upper part in the Center of the ceiling; in the midst, instead of a Tombstone, was a round Altar covered

9

over with a plate of brass, and thereon this engraving:

A.C. R.C. Hoc universi compendium unius mihi sepulchrum feci.

Round about the first Circle or Brim stood, *Jesus mihi omnia.*

In the center were four figures, enclosed in circles, whose circumscription was,

1. *Nequaquam vacuum.*
2. *Legis Jugum.*
3. *Libertas Evangeli.*
4. *Dei gloria intacta.*

This is all clear and bright, as also the seventh side and the two Heptagoni: so we kneeled altogether down, and gave thanks to the sole wise, sole mighty, and sole eternal God, who had taught us more then all men's wit could have found out, praised be his holy name. This Vault we parted in three parts, the upper part or ceiling, the wall or side, the ground or floor.

Of the upper part you shall understand no more of it at this time, but that it was divided according to the seven sides in the triangle, which was in the bright center; but what therein is contained, you shall God willing (that are desirous of our society) behold the same with your own eyes; but every side or wall is parted into ten squares, everyone with their several figures and sentences, as they are truly showed, and set forth Concentratum here in our book.

The bottom again is parted in the triangle, but because therein is described the power and rule of the inferior Governors, we leave to manifest the same, for fear of the abuse by the evil and ungodly world. But those that are provided and stored with the heavenly Antidote, they do without fear or hurt, tread on, and bruise the head of the old and evil serpent, which this our age is well fitted for: every side or wall had a door for a chest, wherein there lay diverse things, especially all our books, which otherwise we had, besides the *Vocabular of Theoph: Par. Ho.* and these which daily we do participate. Herein also we found his *Itinerarium*, and *vitam*, whence this relation for the most part is taken. In another chest were looking glasses of divers virtues, as also in other places were little bells, burning lamps, & chiefly wonderful artificial Songs; generally all done to that end, that if it should happen after many hundred years, the Order or Fraternity should come to nothing, they might by this Vault be restored again.

Now as yet we had not seen the dead body of our careful and wise father, we therefore removed the Altar aside, there we lifted up a strong plate of brass, and found a fair and worthy body, whole and unconsumed, as the same is here lively counterfeited, with all the Ornaments and Attires; in his hand he held a parchment book, called I. the which next to the Bible, is our greatest treasure, which ought to be delivered to the censure of the world.

At the end of this book stands this following Elogium.

Granum pectori Jesu insitum.

C. Ros. C. ex nobili atque splendida Germaniae R.C. familia oriundus, vir sui seculi divinis revelationibus subtilissimis imaginationibus, indefessis laboribus ad coelestia, atque humana mysteria ; arcanave admissus postquam suam (quam Arabico, & Africano itineribus Collegerat) plusquam regiam, atque imperatoriam Gazam suo seculo nondum convenientem, posteritati eruendam custo divisset et jam suarum Artium, ut et nominis, fides acconjunctissimos herides instituisset, mundum minutum omnibus motibus magno illi respondentem fabricasset hocque tandem preteritarum, praesentium, et futurarum, rerum compendio extracto, centenario major non morbo (quem ipse nunquam corpore expertus erat, nunquam alios infestare sinebat) ullo pellente sed spiritu Dei evocante, illuminatam animam (inter Fratrum amplexus et ultima oscula) fidelissimo creatori Deo reddidisset, Pater dilectissimus, Fra: suavissimus, praeceptor fidelissimus amicus integerimus, a suis ad 120 annos hic absconditus est.

Underneath they had subscribed themselves,

1. Fra: I.A. Fr. C.H. *electione Fraternitatis caput.*
2. Fr: G.V. M.P.C.
3. Fra: R.C. *Iunior haeres S. spiritus.*
4. Fra: B.M. P.A. *Pictor et Architectus.*
5. Fr: G.G. M.P.I. *Cabalista.*

Secundi Circuli.
1. Fra: P.A. *Successor,* Fr: I.O. *Mathematicus.*
2. Fra: A. *Successor,* Fra. P.D.
3. Fra: R. *Successor patris* C.R.C. *cum Christo triumphant.*

At the end was written:

Ex Deo Nascimur, in Jesu morimur, per
spiritum sanctum reviviscimus.

At that time was already dead Brother I.O. and Fra: D. but their burial place where is it to be found? We doubt not but our Fra: Senior had the same, and some

11

especial thing laid in Earth, and perhaps likewise hidden: we also hope that this our Example will stir up others more diligently to enquire after their names (whom we have therefore published) and to search for the place of their burial; for the most part of them, by reason of their practice and physick, are yet known, and praised among very old folks; so might perhaps our Gaza be enlarged, or at least be better cleared.

Concerning *Minitum Mundum,* we found it kept in another little Altar, truly more improved than can be imagined by any understanding man; but we will leave him unidentified, until we shall truly be answered upon this our true hearted Famam; and so we have covered it again with the plates, and set the altar thereon, shut the door, and made it sure, with all our seals; besides by instruction and command of our Rota, there are come to sight some books, among which is contained M. (which were made instead of household care by the praiseworthy M.P.) Finally, we departed the one from the other, and left the natural heirs in possession of our Jewels. And so, we do expect the answer and judgment of the learned, or unlearned.

How can we know that after a time if there will be a general reformation, both of divine and humane things, according to our desire, and the expectation of others: for it's fitting, that before the rising of the Sun, there should appear and break forth Aurora, or some clearness, or divine light in the sky; and so in the mean time some few, which shall give their names, may join together, thereby to increase the number and respect of our Fraternity, and make a happy and wished for beginning of our Philosophical Canons, prescribed to us by our brother R.C. and be partakers with us of our treasures (which never can fail or be wasted) in all humility, and love to be eased of this worlds labor, and not walk so blindly in the knowledge of the wonderful works of God.

But that also every Christian may know of what Religion and belief we are, we confess to have the knowledge of Jesus Christ (as the same now in these last days, and chiefly in Germany, most clear and pure is professed, and is today cleansed and void of all swerving people, Hereticks, and false Prophets) in certain and noted Countries maintained, defended and propagated: Also we use two Sacraments, as they are instituted with all Forms and Ceremonies of the first renewed Church. In *Politia,* we recognize the Roman Empire and *Quartam Monarchiam* for our Christian head; albeit we know what alterations be at hand, and would fain impart the same with all our hearts, to other godly learned men; notwithstanding our handwriting which is in our hands, no man (except God alone) can make it common, nor any unworthy person is able to bereave us of it. But we shall help with secret aid this so good a cause, as God shall permit or hinder us: For our God is not blind, as the Heathens Fortuna, but is the Churches Ornament, and the honor of the Temple. Our Philosophy also is not a new Invention, but as Adam after his fall had received it, and as Moses and Solomon used it:

12

also she ought not much to be doubted of, or contradicted by other opinions, or meanings; but seeing the truth is peaceable, brief, and always like herself in all things, and especially accorded by with Jesus in *omni parte* and all members. And as he is the true Image of the Father, so is she his Image; It shall not be said, this is true according to Philosophy, but true according to Theology; and wherein Plato, Aristotle, Pythagoras and others did hit the mark, and wherein Enoch, Abraham, Moses, Solomon did excel; but especially wherewith that wonderful book the Bible agree. All that same occurs together, and make a Sphere or Globe, whose total parts are equidistant from the Center, as hereof more at large and plainer shall be spoken of in Christianly Conference.

But now concerning (and chiefly in this our age) the ungodly and accursed Gold-making, which had gotten so much the upper-hand, whereby under color of it, many runagates and roguish people do use great villainies, and cozen and abuse the credit, which is given them: yea nowadays men of discretion do hold the transmutation of Metals to be the highest point, and zenith in Philosophy, this is all their intent, and desire, and that God would be most esteemed by them, and honored, which could make great store of Gold, and in abundance, the which with unpremeditated prayers, they hope to attain of the all-knowing God, and searcher of all hearts: we therefore do by these presents publicly testify, that the true Philosophers are far of another mind, esteeming little the making of Gold, which is but a paragon; for besides that they have a thousand better things.

And we say with our loving Father R.C.C. *Phy: aureum nisi quantum aurum,* for unto them the whole nature is detected: he does not rejoice, that he can make Gold, and that, as said Christ, the devils are obedient unto him; but is glad that he sees the Heavens open, and the Angels of God ascending and descending, and his name written in the book of life. Also we do testify that under the name of Chymia many books and pictures are set forth in *Contumeliam gloriae Dei,* as we will name them in their due season, and will give to the pure-hearted a Catalogue, or Register of them: And we pray all learned men to take heed of these kind of Books; for the enemy never rested, but sowed his weeds, til a stronger one does root it out. So according to the will and meaning of Fra: C.R.C. we his brethren request again all the learned in Europe, who shall read (sent forth in five languages) this our *Famam* and *Confessionem,* that it would please them with good deliberation to ponder this our offer, and to examine most nearly and most sharply their Arts, and behold the present time with all diligence, and to declare their mind, either *Cummunicate consilio,* or singulatim by Print.

And although at this time we make no mention either of our names, or meetings, yet nevertheless every ones opinion shall assuredly come to our hands, in what language so ever it be; nor any body shall fail, who so gives but his name to speak with some of us, either by word of mouth, or else if there be some letter in writing.

And this we say for a truth, That whosoever shall earnestly, and from his heart, bear affection unto us, it shall be beneficial to him in goods, body and soul; but he that is false-hearted, or greedy of riches, the same first of all shall not be able in any manner of wise to hurt us, but bring him to utter ruin and destruction. Also, our building (although one hundred thousand people had very near seen and beheld the same) shall for ever remain untouched, undestroyed, and hidden to the wicked world, *sub umbra alarum tuarum Jehova.* [Under the shadow of your wings, *Jehova*]

Confessio Fraternitatis

Anonymous, 1615
the second Rosicrucian Manifesto

Confessio Fraternitatis, or The Confession of the Laudable Fraternity of the Most Honorable
Order of the Rosy Cross, Written to All the Learned of Europe

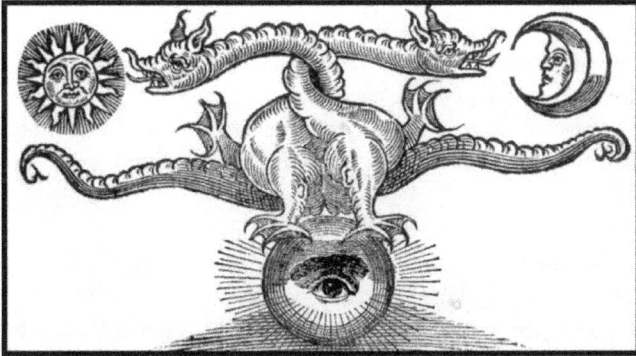

Whatsoever is published, and made known to everyone, concerning our Fraternity, by the foresaid *Fama*, let no man esteem lightly of it, nor hold it as an idle or invented thing, and much less receive the same, as though it were only a mere conceit of ours. It is the Lord Jehovah (who seeing the Lord's Sabbath is almost at hand, and hastened again, his period or course being finished, to his first beginning) does turn about the course of Nature; and what heretofore had been sought with great pains, and daily labor, is now manifested unto those who make small account, or scarcely once think upon it; but those which desire it, it is in a manner forced and thrust upon them, that thereby the life of the godly may be eased of all their toil and labor, and be no more subject to the storms of inconstant Fortune; but the wickedness of the ungodly thereby, with their due and deserved punishment, be augmented and multiplied.

Although we cannot be by any suspected of the least heresy, or of any wicked beginning, or purpose against the worldly government, we do condemn the East and the West (meaning the Pope and Mahomet) blasphemers against our Lord Jesus Christ, and offer and present with a good will to the chief head of the Roman Empire our prayers, secrets, and great treasures of gold.

Yet we have thought good, and fit for the educated, to add somewhat more to this, and make a better explanation if there be anything too deep, hidden, and set

15

down over dark in the *Fama*, or for certain reasons were altogether omitted, and left out; hoping herewith the learned will be more addicted unto us, and be made far more fit and willing for our purpose.

Concerning the alteration and amendment of Philosophy, we have (as much as this present is needful) sufficiently declared, to wit, that the same is altogether weak and faulty; yet we doubt not, although the most part falsely do allege that she (I know not how) is sound and strong, yet notwithstanding she fetches her last breath and is departing.

But as commonly, even in the same place or country where there broke forth a new a unaccustomed disease, Nature also there discovered a medicine against the same; so there does appear for so manifold infirmities of Philosophy the right means, and unto our Patria sufficiently offered, whereby she may become sound again, which is now to be renewed and altogether new.

No other Philosophy we have, than that which is the head and sum, the foundations and contents of all faculties, sciences, and arts, the which (if we will behold our age) contained much of Theology and medicine, but little of the wisdom of the law, and does diligently search both heaven and earth: or, to speak briefly thereof, which does manifest and declare sufficiently Man, whereof all learned who will make themselves known unto us, and come into our brotherhood, shall find more wonderful secrets by us than heretofore they did attain unto, and did know, or are able to believe or utter.

Wherefore, to declare briefly our meaning hereof, we ought to labor carefully that there be not only a wondering at our meeting and adoration, but that likewise everyone may know, that although we do not lightly esteem and regard such mysteries and secrets, we nevertheless hold it fit, that the knowledge thereof be manifested and revealed to many.

For it is to be taught and believed, that this our undesired (for), willing offer will raise many and divers thoughts in men, unto whom (as yet) be unknown Miranda *sexta aetatis*, or those which by reason of the course of the world, esteem the things to come like unto the present, and are hindered through all manner of importunities of this our time, so that they live no otherwise in the world, than blind fools, who can, in the clear sunshine day discern and know nothing, than only by feeling.

Confessio Fraternitatis

Now concerning the first part, we maintain that the meditations, knowledge and inventions of our loving Christian Father *(of all that, which from the beginning of the world,*

Man's wisdom, either through God's revelation, or through the service of the angels and spirits, or through the sharpness and depth of understanding, or through long observation, use, and experience, had found out, invented, brought forth, corrected, and till now had been propagated and transplanted) are so excellent, worthy and great, that if all books should perish, and by God's almighty sufferance, all writings and all teachings should be lost, yet the posterity will be able only thereby to lay a new foundation, and bring truth to light again; the which perhaps would not be so hard to do as if one should begin to pull down and destroy the old ruinous building, and then to enlarge the fore court, afterwards bring lights into the lodgings, and then change the doors, stair, and other things according to our intention.

But to whom would not this be acceptable, for to be manifested to everyone rather that to have it kept and spared, as an especial ornament for the appointed time to come?

Wherefore should we not with all our hearts rest and remain in the only truth (which men through so many erroneous and crooked ways do seek) if it had only pleased God to lighten unto us the sixth *Candelbrium*? Was it not good that we needed not to care, not to fear hunger, poverty, sickness and age?

Was it not a precious thing, that you could always live so, as if you had lived from the beginning of the world, and, moreover, as you should still live to the end thereof? Was it not excellent you dwell in one place, that neither the people which dwell beyond the River Ganges in the Indies could Hide anything, nor those which in Peru might be able to keep secret their counsels from you?

Were it not a precious thing, that you could so read in one only book, and withal by reading understand and remember, all that which in all other books (which heretofore have been, and are now, and hereafter shall come out) had been, is, and shall be learned and found out of them?

How pleasant were it, that you could so sing, that instead of stony rocks you could draw the pearls and precious stones, instead of wild beasts, spirits, and instead of hellish Pluto, move the might princes of the world.

O you people, God's counsel is far otherwise, who had concluded now to increase and enlarge the number of our Fraternity, the which we with such joy have undertaken, as we have heretofore obtained this great treasure without our merits, yea without our hopes, and thoughts, and purpose with the like fidelity to put the same in practice, that neither the compassion nor pity of our own children (which some of us in the Fraternity have) shall draw us from it, because we know these unhoped for goods

17

cannot be inherited, nor by chance be obtained.

If there be somebody now, which on the other side will complain of our discretion, that we offer our treasure so freely, and without any difference to all men, and do not rather regard and respect more the godly, learned, wise, or princely persons, than the common people; those we do not contradict, seeing it is not a slight and easy matter; but withal we signify so much, that our *Arcana* or secrets will no ways be common, and generally made known. Although the *Fama* be set forth in five languages, and is manifested to everyone, yet we do partly very well know that the unlearned and gross wits will not receive nor regard the same; as also the worthiness of those who shall be accepted into our Fraternity are not esteemed and known of us by Man's carefulness, but by the Rule of our Revelation and Manifestation. Wherefore if the unworthy cry and call a thousand times, or if they shall offer and present themselves to us a thousand times, yet God had commanded our ears, that they should hear none of them: yea God had so compassed us about with his clouds, that unto us his servants no violence or force can be done or committed; wherefore we neither can be seen or known by anybody, except he had the eyes of an eagle. It had been necessary that the *Fama* be set forth in everyone's mother tongue, because those should not be defrauded of the knowledge thereof, whom (although they be unlearned) God had not excluded from the happiness of this Fraternity, the which shall be divided and parted into certain degrees; as those which dwell in the city of Damascus in Arabia, who have a far different politick order from the other Arabians. For there govern only wise and understanding men, who by the king's permission make particular laws; according unto which example also the government shall be instituted in Europe (whereof we have a description set down by our Christianly Father) when first is done and come to pass that which is to precede. And thenceforth our Trumpet shall publicly sound with a loud sound, and great noise, when namely the same (which at this present is shown by few, and is secretly, as a thing to come, declared in figures and pictures) shall be free and publicly proclaimed, and the whole world shall be filled withal. Even in such manner as heretofore, many godly people have secretly and altogether desperately pushed at the Pope's tyranny, which afterwards, with great, earnest, and especial zeal in Germany, was thrown from his seat, and trodden underfoot, whose final fall is delayed, and kept for our times, when he also shall be scratched in pieces with nails, and an end be made of his ass's cry, by a new voice. The which we know is already reasonable manifest and known to many learned men in Germany, as their writings and secret congratulations do sufficiently witness the same.

We could here relate and declare what all the time, from the year of Our Lord 1378 (in which year our Christian Father was born) till now, had happened, where we might rehearse what alterations he had seen in these one hundred and six years of his life, which he had left to our brethren and us after his decease to peruse. But brevity, which we do observe, will not permit at this present to make rehearsal of it, till a more fit time. At this time, it is enough for those which do not despise our declaration, having therefore briefly touched it, thereby to prepare the way for their acquaintance and friendship with us.

Yet to whom it is permitted that he may perceive, and for his instruction use, those great letters and characters which the Lord god had written and imprinted in heaven and earth's edifice, through the alteration of government, which had been from time to time altered and reviewed, the same is already (although as yet unknown to himself) ours. And as we know he will not despise our inviting and calling, so none shall fear any deceit, for we promise and openly say, that no man's uprightness and hopes shall deceive him, whosoever shall make himself known unto us under the seal of secrecy, and desire our Fraternity.

But to the false hypocrites, and to those that seek other things than wisdom, we say and witness by these presents publicly, we cannot be made known, and be betrayed unto them; and much less they shall be able to hurt as any manner of way without the will of God; but they shall certainly be partakers of all the punishment spoken of in our *Fama*; so their wicked counsels shall light upon themselves, and our treasures shall remain untouched and unstirred, until the Lion does come, who will ask them for his use, and employ them for the confirmation and establishment of his kingdom. We ought therefore here to observe well, and make it known unto everyone, that God had certainly and most assuredly concluded to send and grant to the world before her end, which presently thereupon shall ensue, such a truth, light, life, and glory, as the first man Adam had, which he lost in Paradise, after which his successors were put and driven, with him, to misery. Wherefore there shall cease all servitude, falsehood, lies, and darkness, which by little and little, with the great world's revolution, was crept into all arts, works, and governments of men, and have darkened the most part of them. For form thence are proceeded an innumerable sort of all manner of false opinions and heresies, that scarce the wisest of all was able to know whose doctrine and opinion he should follow and embrace, and could not well and easily be discerned; seeing on the one part they were detained, hindered, and brought into errors through the respect of the philosophers and learned men, and on the other part through true experience. All the which, when it shall once be abolished and removed, and instead thereof a right and true rule instituted, then there will remain thanks unto them which have taken pains therein. But the work itself shall be attributed to the blessedness of our age.

As we now willingly confess, that may principal men by their writings will be a great furtherance unto this Reformation which is to come; so, we desire not to have this honor ascribed to us, as if such work were only commanded and imposed upon us. But we confess, and witness openly with the Lord Jesus Christ, that it shall first happen that the stones shall arise, and offer their service, before there shall be any want of executors and accomplishers of God's counsel; yea, the Lord God had already sent before certain messengers, which should testify his will, to wit, some new stars, which do appear and are seen in the firmament in *Serpentario* and *Cygno*, which signify and give themselves known to everyone, that they are powerful *Signacula* of great weighty matters. So then, the secret his writings and characters are most necessary for all such things which are found out by men. Although that great book of nature stands open to all men, yet there are but few that can read and understand the same. For as there is given to man two instruments to hear, likewise two to see, and two to smell, but only one to speak, and it were but vain to expect speech from the ears or hearing from the eyes. So, there had been ages or times which have seen, there have also been ages that have heard, smelt, and tasted. Now there remains yet that which in short time, honor shall be likewise given to the tongue, and by the same; what before times had been seen, heard, and smelt, now finally shall be spoken and uttered forth, when the World shall awake out of her heavy and drowsy sleep, and with an open heart, bare-head, and barefoot, shall merrily and joyfully meet the new arising Sun.

These characters and letters, as God had here and there incorporated them in the Holy Scriptures, the Bible, so had he imprinted them in all beasts. So that like as the mathematician and astronomer can long before see and know the eclipses which are to come, so we may verily foreknow and foresee the darkness of obscurations of the Church, and how long they shall last. From the which characters or letters, we have borrowed our magic writing, and have found out, and made, a new language for ourselves, in the which withal is expressed and declared the nature of all things. So that it is no wonder that we are not so eloquent in other languages, the which we know that they are altogether disagreeing to the language of our forefathers, Adam and Enoch, and were through the Babylonical confusion wholly hidden.

But we must also let you understand that there are yet some Eagles' Feathers in our way, the which do hinder our purpose. Wherefore we do admonish everyone for to read diligently and continually the Holy Bible, for he that takes all his pleasures therein, he shall know that he prepared for himself an excellent way to come to our Fraternity. For as this is the whole sum and content of our rule, that every letter or character which is in the world ought to be learned and regarded well; so those are like unto us, and are very near allied unto us, who do make the Holy Bible a rule of their life, and an aim and end of all their studies: yea to let it be a compendium and content of the whole world. And not only to have it continually in the mouth, but to know how to apply and direct the true understanding of it to all times and ages of the world. Also, it is not our custom to prostitute and make so common the Holy Scriptures; for there are innumerable expounders of the same; some alleging and wresting it to serve for their opinion, some to scandal it, and most wickedly do like it to a nose of wax, which alike should serve the divines, philosophers, physicians, and mathematicians, against all the which we do openly witness and acknowledge, that from the beginning of the world there had not been given unto men a more worthy, a more excellent, and more admirable and wholesome Book than the Holy Bible. Blessed is he that had the same, yet more blessed is he who reads it diligently, but most blessed of all is he that truly understands the same, for he is most like to God, and does truly understand the same, for his most like to God, and does come most near to him. But whatsoever had been said in the *Fama* concerning the deceivers against the transmutation of metals, and the highest medicine in the world, the same is thus to be understood, that this so great gift of God we do in no manner set at naught or despise it. But because she brings not with her always the knowledge of Nature, but this brings forth not only medicine, but also manifests and opens unto us innumerable secrets and wonders. Therefore, it is requisite, that we be earnest to attain to the understanding and knowledge of philosophy. And moreover, excellent wits ought not to be drawn to the tincture of metals, before they be exercised well in the knowledge of Nature. He must needs be an insatiable creature, who is come so far, that neither poverty nor sickness can hurt him, yea, who is exalted above all other men, and had rule over that, the which does anguish, trouble and pain others, yet will give himself again to idle things, as to build houses, make wars, and use all manner of pride, because he had gold and silver infinite store.

God is far otherwise pleased, for he exalted the lowly, and pulled down the proud with disdain; to those which are of few works, he sent His Holy Angel to speak with them, but the unclean babblers he drove into the wilderness and solitary places. The which is the right reward of the Romish seducers, who have vomited forth their blasphemies against Christ, and yet do not abstain from their lies in this clear shining light. In Germany, all their abominations and detestable tricks have been disclosed, that thereby he may fully fulfill the measure of sin and draw near to the end of his punishment. Therefore one day it will come to pass, that the mouth of those vipers will be stopped, and the triple crown will be brought to naught, as thereof at our meeting shall plainer and at large be discoursed.

For conclusion of our Confession, we must earnestly admonish you, that you put away, if not all, yet the most books written by false Alchemists, who do think it but a jest, or a pastime, when they either misuse the Holy Trinity, when they do apply it to vain things, or deceive the people with most strange figures, and dark sentences and speeches, and cozen the simple of their money; as there are nowadays too many such books set forth, which the Enemy of man's welfare does daily, and will to the end, mingle among the good seed, thereby to make the Truth more difficult to be believed, which in herself is simple, easy, and naked, but contrarily Falsehood is proud, haughty, and colored with a kind of luster of seeming godly and of humane wisdom. You that are wise eschew such books, and turn unto us, who seek not your moneys, but offer unto you most willingly our great treasures. We hunt not after your goods with invented lying tinctures, but desire to make you partakes of our goods. We speak unto you by parables, but would willingly bring you to the right, simple, easy and ingenuous exposition, understanding, declaration, and knowledge of all secrets. We desire not to be received by you, but invite you unto our more than kingly houses and palaces, and that verily not by our own proper motion, but (that you likewise may know it) as forced unto it, by the instigation of the Spirit of God, by his admonitions, and by the occasion of this present time.

What think you, loving people, and how seem you affected, seeing that you now understand and know, that we acknowledge ourselves truly and sincerely to profess Christ, condemn the Pope, addict ourselves to the true Philosophy, lead a Christian life, and daily call, entreat and invite many more unto our Fraternity, unto whom the same Light of God likewise appeared? Consider not at length how you might begin with us, not only by pondering the Gifts which are in you, and by experience which you have in the word of God, beside the careful consideration of the imperfection of all arts, and many other unfitting things, to seek for an amendment therein; to appease God, and to accommodate you for the time wherein you live. Certainly if you will perform the same, this profit will follow, that all those goods which Nature had in all parts of the world wonderfully dispersed, shall at one time altogether be given unto you, and shall easily disburden you of all that which obscured the understanding of man, and hindered the working thereof, like unto the vain eccentrics and epicycles.

But those pragmatic and busy-headed men, who either are blinded with the glittering of gold, or (to say more truly) who are now honest, but by; thinking such great riches should never fail, might easily be corrupted, and brought to idleness, and to riotous proud living, those we desire that they would not trouble us with their idle and vain crying. But let them think, that although there be a medicine to be had which might fully cure all diseases, nevertheless those whom God had destined to plague with diseases, nevertheless those whom God had destined to plaque with diseases, and to keep under the rod of correction, such shall never obtain any such medicine.

Even in such manner, although we might enrich the whole world, and endue them with learning, and might release it from innumerable miseries, yet shall we never be manifested and made known unto any many, without the especial pleasure of God; yea, it shall be so far from him whosoever thinks to get the benefit and be partaker of our riches and knowledge, without and against the will of God, that he shall sooner lose his life in seeking and searching for us, than to find us, and attain to come to the wished happiness of the Fraternity of the Rosy Cross.

The Chymical Wedding
of
Christian Rosenkreutz

Anonymous, 1616
the Third Rosicrucian Manifesto

The First Day

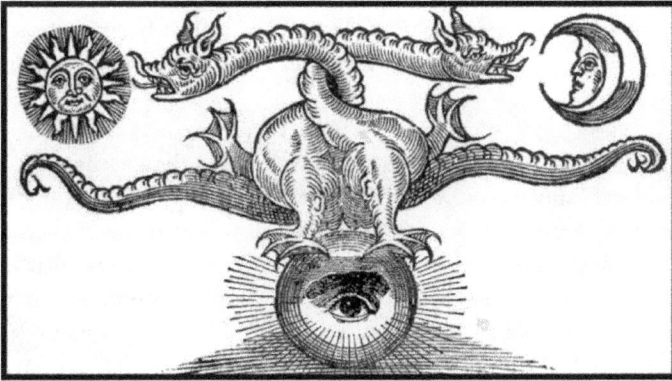

On an evening before Easter, I sat at a table, and having (as my custom was) in my humble prayer sufficiently conversed with my Creator, and considered many great mysteries (whereof the Father of Lights his Majesty had shown me not a few) and being now ready to prepare in my heart, together with my dear Paschal Lamb, a small, unleavened, undefiled cake; all of a sudden arose so horrible a tempest, that I imagined no other but that through its mighty force, the hill on which my little house was founded would fly into pieces.

But inasmuch as this, and the like from the Devil (who had done me many a spite) was no new thing to me, I took courage, and persisted in my meditation, till somebody in an unusual manner touched me on the back; whereupon I was so hugely terrified, that I dared hardly look about me; yet I showed myself as cheerful as (in such occurrences) human frailty would permit. Now the same thing still

23

twitching me several times by the coat, I looked back, and behold it was a fair and glorious lady, whose garments were all sky-colored, and curiously (like Heaven) bespangled with golden stars; in her right hand she bore a trumpet of beaten gold, on which a Name was engraved which I could well read but am as yet forbidden to reveal it. In her left hand she had a great bundle of letters of all languages, which she (as I afterwards understood) was to carry to all countries. She also had large and beautiful wings, full of eyes throughout, with which she could mount aloft, and fly swifter than any eagle.

I might perhaps have been able to take further notice of her, but because she stayed so little time with me, and terror and amazement still possessed me, I had to be content. For as soon as I turned about, she turned her letters over and over, and at length drew out a small one, which with great reverence she laid down upon the table, and without giving one word, departed from me. But in her mounting upward, she gave so mighty a blast on her gallant trumpet, that the whole hill echoed from it, and for a full quarter of an hour after, I could hardly hear my own words.

In so unlooked for an adventure I was at a loss, how either to advise or to assist my poor self, and therefore fell upon my knees and besought my Creator to permit nothing contrary to my eternal happiness to befall me. Whereupon with fear and trembling, I went to the letter, which was now so heavy, that had it been mere gold it could hardly have been so weighty. Now as I was diligently viewing it, I found a little seal, on which a curious cross with this inscription, *IN HOC SIGNO VINCES*, was engraved.

Now as soon as I espied this sign I was the more comforted, as not being ignorant that such a seal was little acceptable, and much less useful, to the Devil. Whereupon I tenderly opened the letter, and within it, in an azure field, in golden letters, found the following verses written.

This day, today
Is the Royal Wedding day.
For this thou were born
And chosen of God for delight
Thou may go to the mountain
Whereon three temples stand,
And see there this affair.

Keep watch
Examine yourself

24

And you should bathe thoroughly
The Wedding may bring you harm.
Trouble comes to him who fails here.
Let him be careful of who is too light.

Below was written: Sponsus and Sponsa.

As soon as I had read this letter, I was presently like to have fainted away, all my hair stood on end, and a cold sweat tricked down my whole body. For although I well perceived that this was the appointed wedding, of which seven years before I was acquainted in a bodily vision, and which now for so long a time I had with great earnestness awaited, and which lastly, by the account and calculation of the planets, I had most diligently observed, I found so to be, yet could I never foresee that it must happen under such grievous perilous conditions. For whereas I before imagined, that to be a welcome and acceptable guest, I needed only to be ready to appear at the wedding, I was now directed to Divine Providence, of which until this time I was never certain.

I also found by myself, the more I examined myself, that in my head there was nothing but gross misunderstanding, and blindness in mysterious things, so that I was not able to comprehend even those things which lay under my feet, and which I daily conversed with, much less that I should be born to the searching out and understanding of the secrets of Nature, since in my opinion Nature might everywhere find a more virtuous disciple, to whom to entrust her precious, though temporary and changeable, treasures.

I found also that my bodily behavior, and outward good conversation, and brotherly love towards my neighbor, was not duly purged and cleansed. Moreover the tickling of the flesh manifested itself, whose affection was bent only to pomp and bravery, and worldly pride, and not to the good of mankind: and I was always contriving how by this art I might in a short time abundantly increase my profit and advantage, rear up stately palaces, make myself an everlasting name in the world, and other similar carnal designs. But the obscure words concerning the three temples particularly afflicted me, which I was not able to make out by any after-speculation, and perhaps should not have done so yet, had they not been wonderfully revealed to me.

Thus stuck between hope and fear, examining myself again and again, and finding only my own frailty and impotence, not being in any way able to succor myself, and exceedingly amazed at the fore mentioned threatening, at length I betook myself to my usual and most secure course — after I had finished my earnest and most fervent prayer, I laid myself down in my bed, so that perchance my good angel by the Divine permission might appear, and (as it had sometimes formerly happened) instruct me in this doubtful affair. Which to the praise of God, my own good, and my neighbors' faithful and hearty warning and amendment, did now likewise come about.

For I was yet scarcely fallen asleep, when I thought that I, together with an innumerable multitude of men, lay fettered with great chains in a dark dungeon, in which, without the least glimpse of light, we swarmed like bees one over another, and thus rendered each other's affliction more grievous. But although neither I nor any of the rest could see one jot, yet I continually heard one heaving himself above the other, when his chains and fetters had become ever so slightly lighter, though none of us had much reason to shove up above the other, since we were all captive wretches.

Now when I with the rest had continued a good while in this affliction, and each was still reproaching the other with his blindness and captivity, at length we heard many trumpets sounding together and kettle drums beating in such a masterly fashion, that it even revived us in our calamity and made us rejoice.

During this noise the cover of the dungeon was lifted up from above, and a little light let down to us. Then first might truly have been discerned the bustle we kept, for all went pell-mell, and he who perchance had heaved himself up too much, was forced down again under the others' feet. In brief, each one strove to be uppermost. Neither did I myself linger, but with my weighty fetters slipped up from under the rest, and then heaved myself upon a stone, which I laid hold of; howbeit, I was caught at several times by others, from whom yet as well as I might, I still guarded myself with hands and feet. For we imagined no other but that we should all be set at liberty, which yet fell out quite otherwise.

For after the nobles who looked upon us from above through the hole had recreated themselves a while with our struggling and lamenting, a certain hoary-headed ancient man called to us to be quiet, and having scarcely obtained this, began (as I still remember) to speak on thus:

If poor humankind
Were not so proud
It would have been given much good
From my Mother's heritage,
But because the humans will not take heed
It lies in such straits
And must be held in prison.

26

And yet my dearest Mother
Will not regard their mischief,
She leaves her beautiful gifts
That many a man might come to the light,
Though this may chance but seldom
That they be better prized
Nor reckoned as only a story.

Therefore, in honor of the feast
Which we shall hold today,
That her grace may be multiplied
A fine work will she do:
The rope will now be lowered
Whoever may hang on to it
He shall be unchained.

He had scarcely finished speaking when an ancient matron commanded her servants to let down the cord seven times into the dungeon and draw up whosoever could hang upon it. Good God! that I could sufficiently describe the hurry and disquiet that then arose amongst us; for everyone strove to get to the cord, and yet only hindered each other. But after seven minutes a sign was given by a little bell, whereupon at the first pull the servants drew up four. At that time, I could not get very near the cord, having (as is before mentioned) to my huge misfortune, betaken myself to a stone at the wall of the dungeon; and thereby I was made unable to get to the cord which descended in the middle.

The cord was let down the second time, but many, because their chains were too heavy, and their hands too tender, could not keep their hold on the cord, but with themselves beat down many another who else perhaps might have held fast enough; nay, many a one was forcibly pulled off by another, who yet could not himself get at it, so mutually envious were we even in this our great misery.

But they of all others most moved my compassion whose weight was so heavy that they tore their very hands from their bodies, and yet could not get up. Thus, it came to pass that at those five times very few were drawn up. For as soon as the sign was given, the servants were so nimble at drawing the cord up, that the most part tumbled one upon another, and the cord, this time especially, was drawn up very empty.

Whereupon the greatest part, and even I myself, despaired of redemption, and called upon God that he would have pity on us, and (if possible) deliver us out of this obscurity; who then also heard some of us. For when the cord came down

27

the sixth time, some of them hung themselves fast upon it; and whilst being drawn up, the cord swung from one side to the other, and (perhaps by the will of God) came to me, and I suddenly caught it, uppermost above all the rest, and so at length beyond hope came out. At which I rejoiced exceedingly, so that I did not perceive the wound which during the drawing up I had received on my head from a sharp stone, until I, with the rest who were released (as was always done before) had to help with the seventh and last pull; at which time through straining, the blood ran down all over my clothes, which I nevertheless because of my joy did not take notice of. Now when the last drawing up on which the most of all hung was finished, the matron caused the cord to be laid aside, and asked her aged son to declare her resolution to the rest of the prisoners, who after he had thought a little spoke thus unto them.

> *You children dear*
> *You who are here,*
> *It is finished*
> *What long had been known,*
>
> *The great favor which my Mother*
> *Had here shown you twain*
> *You should not disdain:*
> *A joyful time shall soon be come,*
> *When each shall be the other's equal,*
> *No one is poor or rich,*
> *And who was given great commands*
> *Must bring much with him now,*
> *And who was much entrusted with*
> *Stripped to the skin you will be,*
> *Wherefore your lamentations end*
> *Which is after a few days.*

As soon as he had finished these words, the cover was again put to and locked down, and the trumpets and kettle-drums began afresh, yet the noise of them could not be so loud but that the bitter lamentation of the prisoners which arose in the dungeon was heard above all, which soon also caused my eyes to run over.

Presently afterwards the ancient matron, together with her son, sat down on seats before prepared, and commanded the redeemed should be told. Now as soon as she had demanded everyone's name, which were also written down by a little page; having viewed us all, one after another, she sighed, and spoke to her son, so that I could well hear her,

"Ah, how heartily I am grieved for the poor men in the dungeon! I would to God I could release them all."

To which her son replied,

"It is, mother, thus ordained by God, against whom we may not contend. If we were all of us lords, and possessed all the goods upon Earth, and were seated at table, who would there then be to bring up the service?"

Whereupon his mother held her peace, but soon after she said, "Well, however, let these be freed from their fetters," which was likewise presently done, and I was the last except a few; yet I could not refrain (though I still looked upon the rest) but bowed myself before the ancient matron, and thanked God that through her, he had graciously and fatherly vouchsafed to bring me out of such darkness into the light. After me the rest did likewise, to the satisfaction of the matron.

Lastly, to everyone was given a piece of gold for a remembrance, and to spend by the way, on the one side of which was stamped the rising sun, and on the other (as I remember) these three letters, D.L.S.; and therewith everyone had license to depart, and was sent to his own business with this annexed limitation, that we to the glory of God should benefit our neighbors, and reserve in silence what we had been entrusted with; which we also promised to do, and so departed one from another. But because of the wounds which the fetters had caused me, I could not well go forward, but halted on both feet, which the matron presently espying, laughing at it, and calling me again to her said thus to me:

"My son, do not let this defect afflict you, but call to mind your infirmities, and therewith thank God who has permitted you even in this world, and in your state of imperfection, to come into so high a light; and keep these wounds for my sake."

Whereupon the trumpets began to sound again, which gave me such a shock that I woke up, and then first perceived that it was only a dream, but it so strongly impressed my imagination that I was still perpetually troubled about it, and I thought I still felt the wounds on my feet. Howbeit, by all these things I understood well that God had vouchsafed that I should be present at this mysterious and bidden wedding. Wherefore with childlike confidence I returned thanks to his Divine Majesty, and besought him that he would further preserve me in fear of him, that he would daily fill my heart with wisdom and understanding, and at length graciously (without deserting me) conduct me to the desired end.

Hereupon I prepared myself for the way, put on my white linen coat, girded my loins, with a blood-red ribbon bound crossways over my shoulder. In my hat I stuck four red roses, so that I might sooner be noticed amongst the throng by this token. For food I took bread, salt and water, which by the counsel of an understanding person I had at certain times used, not without profit, in similar occurrences.

But before I left my cottage, I first, in this my dress and wedding garment, fell down upon my knees, and besought God that in case such a thing was, he would vouchsafe me a good issue. And thereupon in the presence of God I made a vow that if anything through his grace should be revealed to me, I would employ it to neither my own honor nor my own authority in the world, but to the spreading of his Name, and the service of my neighbor. And with this vow, and good hope, I departed out of my cell with joy.

The Second Day

I had hardly got out of my cell into a forest when I thought the whole heaven and all the elements had already trimmed themselves in preparation for this wedding. For even the birds chanted more pleasantly than before, and the young fawns skipped so merrily that they made my heart rejoice, and moved me to sing; wherefore with a loud voice I thus began:

Rejoice and be happy dear bird
And praise your Maker,
Raise bright and clear your voice,
Your God is most exalted,
Your food he had prepared for you
To give you in due season.
So be content therewith,
Wherefore shall you not be glad,
Wilt thou arraign your God
That he had made you bird?
Wilt trouble your wee head
That he made you not a man?
Be still, he had it well bethought
And be content therewith.
What do I then, a worm of earth
To judge along with God?
That I in this heaven's storm
Do wrestle with all art.

31

You cannot fight with God.
And whoso is not fit for this, let him be sped away
O Man, be satisfied
That he had made you not the King
And take it not amiss,
Perchance had you despised his name,
That were a sorry matter:
For God had clearer eyes that that
He looks into your heart,
You cannot deceive God.

This I sang now from the bottom of my heart throughout the whole forest, so that it resounded from all parts, and the hills repeated my last words, until at length I saw a curious green heath, to which I betook myself out of the forest.

Upon this heath stood three lovely tall cedars, which by reason of their breadth afforded excellent and desired shade, at which I greatly rejoiced. For although I had not hitherto gone far, yet my earnest longing made me very faint, whereupon I hastened to the trees to rest a little under them. But as soon as I came somewhat closer, I saw a tablet fastened to one of them, on which (as afterwards I read) in curious letters the following words were written:

"*God save you, stranger! If you have heard anything concerning the nuptials of the King, consider these words. By us the Bridegroom offers you a choice between four ways, all of which, if you do not sink down in the way, can bring you to his royal court. The first is short but dangerous, and one which will lead you into rocky places, through which it will scarcely be possible to pass. The second is longer, and takes you circuitously; it is plain and easy, if by the help of the Magnet you turn neither to left nor right. The third is that truly royal way which through various pleasures and pageants of our King, affords you a joyful journey; but this so far has scarcely been allotted to one in a thousand. By the fourth no man shall reach the place, because it is a consuming way, practicable only for incorruptible bodies. Choose now which one you will of the three, and persevere constantly therein, for know whichever you will enter, that is the one destined for you by immutable Fate, nor can you go back in it save at great peril to life. These are the things which we would have you know. But, ho, beware! you know not with how much danger you commit yourself to this way, for if you know yourself to be obnoxious by the smallest fault to the laws of our King, I beseech you, while it is still possible, to return swiftly to your house by the way you came.*"

As soon as I read this writing all my joy nearly vanished again, and I who before sang merrily, began now inwardly to lament. For although I saw all the three ways before me, and understood that henceforward it was vouchsafed to me to choose one of them, yet it troubled me that if I went the stony and rocky way, I might get a miserable and deadly fall, or if I took the long one, I might wander out of it through byways, or be in other ways detained in the great journey. Neither could I hope that I amongst thousands should be the very one who should choose the royal way. I saw likewise the fourth before me, but it was so environed with fire and exaltations, that I did not dare draw near it by much, and therefore again and again considered whether I should turn back, or take any of the ways before me. I considered well my own unworthiness, but the dream still comforted me that I was delivered out of the tower; and yet I did not dare confidently rely upon a dream; whereupon I was so perplexed in various ways, that very great weariness, hunger and thirst seized me.

Whereupon I presently drew out my bread and cut a slice of it; which a snow-white dove of whom I was not aware, sitting upon the tree, saw, and therewith (perhaps according to her usual manner) came down. She betook herself very familiarly with me, and I willingly imparted my food to her, which she received, and so with her prettiness she again refreshed me a little. But as soon as her enemy, a most black raven, perceived it, he straight-away darted down upon the dove, and taking no notice of me, would force away the dove's food, and she could not guard herself otherwise than by flight. Whereupon they both flew together towards the south, at which I was so hugely incensed and grieved that without thinking what I did, I hastened after the filthy raven, and so against my will ran into one of the fore mentioned ways a whole field's length. And thus, the raven having been chased away, and the dove delivered, I then first observed what I had inconsiderately done, and that I was already entered into a way, from which under peril of great punishment I could not retire. And though I had still wherewith in some measure to comfort myself, yet that which was worst of all to me was that I had left my bag and bread at the tree and could never retrieve them. For as soon as I turned myself about, a contrary wind was so strong against me that it was ready to knock me down. But if I went forward on the way, I perceived no hindrance at all. From which I could easily conclude that it would cost me my life if I should set myself against the wind, wherefore I patiently took up my cross, got up onto my feet, and resolved, since so it must be, that I would use my utmost endeavor to get to my journey's end before night.

Now although many apparent byways showed themselves, yet I still proceeded with my compass, and would not budge one step from the Meridian Line; howbeit the way was often so rugged and impassable, that I was in no little doubt of it. On this way I constantly thought upon the dove and the raven, and yet could not search out the meaning; until at length upon a high hill afar off I saw a stately portal, to which, not regarding how far it was distant both from me and from the way I was on, I hurried, because the sun had already hid himself under the hills, and I could see no abiding place elsewhere; and this verily I ascribe only to God, who might well have permitted me to go forward in this way, and withheld my eyes that so I might have gazed beside this gate.

To this I now made great haste, and reached it in so much daylight as to take a very competent view of it. Now it was an exceedingly royal beautiful portal, on which were carved a multitude of most noble figures and devices, every one of which (as I afterwards learned) had its peculiar signification. Above was fixed a pretty large tablet, with these words, "*Procul hinc, procul ite profani*" ("keep away, you who are profane"), and other things more, that I was earnestly forbidden to relate.

Now as soon as I came under the portal, there straightaway stepped forth one in a sky-colored habit, whom I saluted in a friendly manner; and though he thankfully returned this salute, yet he instantly demanded of me my letter of invitation. O how glad was I that I had then brought it with me! For how easily I might have forgotten it (as it also chanced to others) as he himself told me!

I quickly presented it, wherewith he was not only satisfied, but (at which I much wondered) showed me abundance of respect, saying, "Come in my brother, you are an acceptable guest to me"; and entreated me not to withhold my name from him. Now I having replied that I was a Brother of the Red-Rosy Cross, he both wondered and seemed to rejoice at it, and then proceeded thus:

"My brother, have you nothing about you with which to purchase a token?"

I answered that my ability was small, but if he saw anything about me he had a mind to, it was at his service. Now he having requested of me my bottle of water, and I having granted it, he gave me a golden token on which stood no more than these two letters, *S.C.*, entreating me that when it stood me in good stead, I would remember him. After which I asked him how many had come in before me, which he also told me, and lastly out of mere friendship gave me a sealed letter to the second Porter.

Now having lingered some time with him, the night grew on. Whereupon a great beacon upon the gates was immediately fired, so that if any were still upon the way, he might make haste thither. But the way, where it finished at the castle, was enclosed on both sides with walls, and planted with all sorts of excellent fruit trees, and on every third tree on each side lanterns were hung up, in which all the candles were lighted with a glorious touch by a beautiful Virgin, dressed in sky-

34

color, which was so noble and majestic a spectacle that I yet delayed somewhat longer than was requisite. But at length after sufficient information, and an advantageous instruction, I departed friendlily from the first Porter.

On the way, I would gladly have known what was written in my letter, yet since I had no reason to mistrust the Porter, and so went on the way, until I came likewise to the second gate, which though it was very like the other, yet it was adorned with images and mystic significations. On the affixed tablet was *"Date et dabitur vobis"* ("give and it shall be given unto you").

Under this gate lay a terrible grim lion chained, who as soon as he saw me arose and made at me with great roaring; whereupon the second Porter who lay upon a stone of marble woke up, and asked me not to be troubled or afraid, and then drove back the lion; and having received the latter which I gave him with trembling, he read it, and with very great respect said thus to me:
"Now welcome in God's Name to me the man who for a long time I would gladly have seen."

Meanwhile he also drew out a token and asked me whether I could purchase it. But having nothing else left but my salt, I presented it to him, which he thankfully accepted. Upon this token again stood only two letters, namely, *S.M.*

I was just about to enter into discourse with him, when it began to ring in the castle, whereupon the Porter counseled me to run, or else all the pains and labor I had hitherto undergone would serve to no purpose, for the lights above were already beginning to be extinguished. Whereupon I went with such haste that I did not heed the Porter, I was in such anguish; and truly it was necessary, for I could not run so fast but that the Virgin, after whom all the lights were put out, was at my heels, and I should never have found the way, had she not given me some light with her torch. I was moreover constrained to enter right next to her, and the gate was suddenly clapped to, so that a part of my coat was locked out, which I was verily forced to leave behind me. For neither I, nor they who stood ready without and called at the gate, could prevail with the Porter to open it again, but he delivered the keys to the Virgin, who took them with her into the court.

Meanwhile I again surveyed the gate, which now appeared so rich that the whole world could not equal it. Just by the door were two columns, on one of which stood a pleasant figure with this inscription, *"Congratulor"*. The other, which had its countenance veiled, was sad, and beneath was written, *"Condoleo"*. In brief, the inscriptions and figures were so dark and mysterious that the most dexterous man on earth could not have expounded them. But all these (if God permits) I shall before long publish and explain.

Under this gate I was again to give my name, which was this last time written down in a little vellum book, and immediately with the rest dispatched to the Lord Bridegroom. It was here where I first received the true guest token, which was somewhat smaller than the former, but much heavier. Upon this stood these letters, *S.P.N.* Besides this, a new pair of shoes were given me, for the floor of the castle was laid with pure shining marble. My old shoes I was to give away to one of the poor who sat in throngs, although in very good order, under the gate. I then bestowed them upon an old man, after which two pages with as many torches conducted me into a little room.

There they asked me to sit down on a form, which I did, but they, sticking their torches in two holes, made in the pavement, departed and thus left me sitting alone. Soon after I heard a noise, but saw nothing, and it proved to be certain men who stumbled in upon me; but since I could see nothing, I had to suffer, and wait to see what they would do with me. But presently perceiving them to be barbers, I entreated them not to jostle me so, for I was content to do whatever they desired; whereupon they quickly let me go, and so one of them (whom I could not yet see) finely and gently cut away the hair round-about from the crown of my head, but over my forehead, ears and eyes he permitted my ice-grey locks to hang. In this first encounter (I must confess) I was ready to despair, for inasmuch as some of them shoved me so forcefully, and yet I could see nothing, I could think nothing other but that God for my curiosity had suffered me to miscarry. Now these invisible barbers carefully gathered up the hair which was cut off and carried it away with them.

After which the two pages entered again, and heartily laughed at me for being so terrified. But they had scarcely spoken a few words with me when again a little bell began to ring, which (as the pages informed me) was to give notice for assembling. Whereupon they asked me to rise, and through many walks, doors and winding stairs lit my way into a spacious hall. In this room was a great multitude of guests, emperors, kings, princes, and lords, noble and ignoble, rich and poor, and all sorts of people, at which I greatly marveled, and thought to myself,' ah, how gross a fool you have been to engage upon this journey with so much bitterness and toil, when (behold) here are even those fellows whom you know well, and yet never had any reason to esteem. They are now all here, and you with all your prayers and supplications have hardly got in at last'. This and more the Devil at that time injected, while I notwithstanding (as well as I could) directed myself to the issue.

Meanwhile one or other of my acquaintance here and there spoke to me:

"Oh Brother Rosencreutz! Are you here too?"

"Yes (my brethren)," I replied, *"the grace of God has helped me in too".*

At which they raised mighty laughter, looking upon it as ridiculous that there should be need of God in so slight an occasion. Now having demanded each of them concerning his way, and finding that most of them were forced to clamber over the rocks, certain trumpets (none of which we yet saw) began to sound to the table, whereupon they all seated themselves, every one as he judged himself above the rest; so that for me and some other sorry fellows there was hardly a little nook left at the lowermost table. Presently the two pages entered, and one of them said grace in so handsome and excellent a manner, that it made the very heart in my body rejoice. However, certain great Sir John's made but little reckoning of them, but jeered and winked at one another, biting their lips within their hats, and using other similar unseemly gestures. After this, meat was brought in, and although no one could be seen, yet everything was so orderly managed, that it seemed to me as if every guest had his own attendant. Now my artists having somewhat recreated themselves, and the wine having removed a little shame from their hearts, they presently began to vaunt and brag of their abilities. One would prove this, another that, and commonly the most sorry idiots made the loudest noise. Ah, when I call to mind what preternatural and impossible enterprises I then heard, I am still ready to vomit at it. In a word, they never kept in their order, but whenever one rascal here, another there, could insinuate himself in between the nobles, then they pretended to having finished such adventures as neither Samson nor yet Hercules with all their strength could ever have achieved: this one would discharge Atlas of his burden; the other would again draw forth the three- headed Cerberus out of Hell. In brief, every man had his own prate, and yet the greatest lords were so simple that they believed their pretences, and the rogues so audacious, that although one or other of them was here and there rapped over the fingers with a knife, yet they flinched not at it, but when anyone perchance had filched a gold-chain, then they would all hazard for the same.

I saw one who heard the rustling of the heavens. The second could see Plato's *Ideas*. A third could number Democritus's atoms. There were also not a few pretenders to the perpetual motion. Many a one (in my opinion) had good understanding, but assumed too much to himself, to his own destruction. Lastly, there was one also who found it necessary to persuade us out of hand that he saw the servitors who attended us, and would have persuaded us as to his contention, had not one of these invisible waiters reached him such a handsome cuff upon his lying muzzle, that not only he, but many more who were by him, became as mute as mice.

But it pleased me most of all, that all those of whom I had any esteem were very quiet in their business, and made no loud cry of it, but acknowledged themselves to be misunderstanding men, to whom the mysteries of nature were too high, and they themselves much too small. In this tumult I had almost cursed the day when I came here; for I could not behold but with anguish that those lewd vain people were above at the board, but I in so sorry a place could not rest in quiet, one of those rascals scornfully reproaching me for a motley fool.

Now I did not realize that there was still one gate through which we must pass, but imagined that during the whole wedding I was to continue in this scorn, contempt and indignity, which I had yet at no time deserved, either from the Lord Bridegroom or the Bride. And therefore (in my opinion) he should have done well to sort out some other fool than me to come to his wedding. Behold, to such impatience the iniquity of this world reduces simple hearts. But this really was one part of my lameness, of which (as is before mentioned) I dreamed. And truly the longer this clamor lasted, the more it increased. For there were already those who boasted of false and imaginary visions, and would persuade us of palpably lying dreams.

Now there sat by me a very fine quiet man, who often discoursed of excellent matters. At length he said, "Behold my brother, if anyone should now come who were willing to instruct these blockish people in the right way, would he be heard?"

"*No, verily*", I replied.

"The world," he said, "*is now resolved (whatever comes of it) to be cheated, and cannot abide to give ear to those who intend its good. Do you see that same cockscomb, with what whimsical figures and foolish conceits he allures others to him? There one makes mouths at the people with unheard-of mysterious words. Yet believe me in this, the time is now coming when those shameful wizards shall be plucked off, and all the world shall know what vagabond impostors were concealed behind them. Then perhaps that will be valued which at present is not esteemed.*"

Whilst he was speaking in this way, and the longer the clamor lasted the worse it was, all of a sudden there began in the hall such excellent and stately music such as I never heard all the days of my life; whereupon everyone held his peace, and waited to see what would become of it. Now in this music there were all the sorts of stringed instruments imaginable, which sounded together in such harmony that I forgot myself, and sat so immovable that those who sat by me were amazed at me; and this lasted nearly half an hour, during which time none of us spoke one word. For as soon as anyone at all was about to open his mouth, he got an unexpected blow, nor did he know where it came from. I thought since we were not permitted to see the musicians, I should have been glad to view just all the instruments they were using. After half an hour this music ceased unexpectedly, and we could neither see nor hear anything more.

Presently after, a great noise began before the door of the hall, with sounding and beating of trumpets, shalms and kettle-drums, as majestic as if the Emperor of Rome had been entering; whereupon the door opened by itself, and then the noise of the trumpets was so loud that we were hardly able to endure it.

Meanwhile (to my thinking) many thousand small tapers came into the hall, all of which themselves marched in so very exact an order as altogether amazed us, till at last the two aforementioned pages with bright torches entered the hall, lighting the way of a most beautiful Virgin, all drawn on a gloriously gilded triumphant self-moving throne. It seemed to me that she was the very same who before on the way kindled and put out the lights, and that these attendants of hers were the very same whom she formerly placed at the trees. She was not now, as before, in sky-color, but arrayed in a snow-white glittering robe, which sparkled with pure gold, and cast such a luster that we could not steadily look at it. Both the pages were dressed in the same manner (although somewhat more modestly). As soon as they came into the middle of the hall, and had descended from the throne, all the small tapers made obeisance before her. Whereupon we all stood up from our benches, yet everyone stayed in his own place. Now she having showed to us, and we again to her, all respect and reverence, in a most pleasant tone she began to speak as follows:

> *The King, my gracious lord*
> *He is not far away,*
> *Nor is his dearest bride, Betrothed to him in honor.*
> *They have now with the greatest joy*
> *Beheld your coming hither.*
> *Wherefore especially they would proffer*
> *Their favor to each one of you,*
> *And they desire from their heart's depth*
> *That you at all times fare you well,*
> *That you have the coming wedding's joy*
> *Unmixed with others' sorrow.*

39

Hereupon with all her small tapers she courteously bowed again, and soon after began as follows:

You know what in the invitation stands:
No man had been called hither
Who had not got from God already
All gifts most beautiful,
And had himself adorned aright
As well befits him here,
Though some may not believe it,
That anyone so wayward be
That on such hard conditions
Should dare to make appearance
When he had not prepared himself
For this wedding long before.
So now they stand in hope
That you be well furnished with all good things,
Be glad that in such hard times
So many folk be found
But men are yet so forward that
They care not for their boorishness
And thrust themselves in places where
They are not called to be.
Let no knave be smuggled in
No rogue slip in with others.
They will declare right openly
That they a wedding pure will have,
So shall upon the morrow's morn
The artist's scales be set
Wherein each one be weighed
And found what he forgotten had.
Of all the host assembled here
Who trusts him not in this
Let him now stand aside.
And should he bide here longer
Then he will lose all grace and favor
Be trodden underfoot,
And he whose conscience pricketh him
Shall be left in this hall today
And by tomorrow he'll be freed
But let him come hither never again.

But he who knows what is behind him
Let him go with his servant
Who shall attend him to his room
And there shall rest him for this day,
For he awaits the scales with praise
Else will his sleep be mighty hard.
Let the others make their comfort here
For he who goes beyond his means
'Twere better he had hid away.
And now the best from each be hoped.

As soon as she had finished saying this, she again made reverence, and sprung cheerfully into her throne, after which the trumpets began to sound again, which yet was not forceful enough to take the grievous sighs away from many. So, they conducted her invisibly away again, but most of the small tapers remained in the room, and one of them accompanied each of us.

In such perturbation it is not possible to express what pensive thoughts and gestures were among us. Yet most of us were resolved to await the scale, and in case things did not work out well, to depart (as they hoped) in peace. I had soon cast up my reckoning, and since my conscience convinced me of all ignorance, and unworthiness, I purposed to stay with the rest in the hall, and chose rather to content myself with the meal I had already taken, than to run the risk of a future repulse. Now after everyone had each been conducted into a chamber (each, as I since understood, into a particular one) by his small taper, there remained nine of us, and among the rest he who discoursed with me at the table too. But although our small tapers did not leave us, yet soon after an hour's time one of the aforementioned pages came in, and, bringing a great bundle of cords with him, first demanded of us whether we had concluded to stay there; when we had affirmed this with sighs, he bound each of us in a particular place, and so went away with our small tapers, and left us poor wretches in darkness.

Then some first began to perceive the imminent danger, and I myself could not refrain from tears. For although we were not forbidden to speak yet anguish and affliction allowed none of us to utter one word. For the cords were so wonderfully made that none could cut them, much less get them off his feet. Yet this comforted me, that still the future gain of many a one who had now taken himself to rest, would prove very little to his satisfaction. But we by only one night's penance might expiate all our presumption. Till at length in my sorrowful thoughts I fell asleep, during which I had a dream. Now although there is no great matter in it, yet I think it not impertinent to recount it.

41

I thought I was upon a high mountain, and saw before me a great and large valley. In this valley were gathered together an unspeakable multitude of people, each of which had at his head a thread, by which he was hanged from Heaven; now one hung high, another low, some stood even almost upon the earth.

But through the air flew up and down an ancient man, who had in his hand a pair of shears, with which he cut here one's, there another's thread. Now he that was close to the earth was so much more ready, and fell without noise, but when it happened to one of the high ones, he fell so that the earth shook. To some it came to pass that their thread was so stretched that they came to the earth before the thread was cut. I took pleasure in this tumbling, and it gave my heart joy, when he who had over-exalted himself in the air about his wedding got so shameful a fall that it even carried some of his neighbors along with him.

In a similar way it also made me rejoice that he who had all this while kept himself near the earth could come down so finely and gently that even the men next to him did not perceive it.

But being now in my highest fit of jollity, I was jogged unawares by one of my fellow captives, upon which I was awakened, and was very much discontented with him. However, I considered my dream, and recounted it to my brother, lying by me on the other side, who was not dissatisfied with it, but hoped that some comfort might be meant by it. In such discourse we spent the remaining part of the night, and with longing awaited the day.

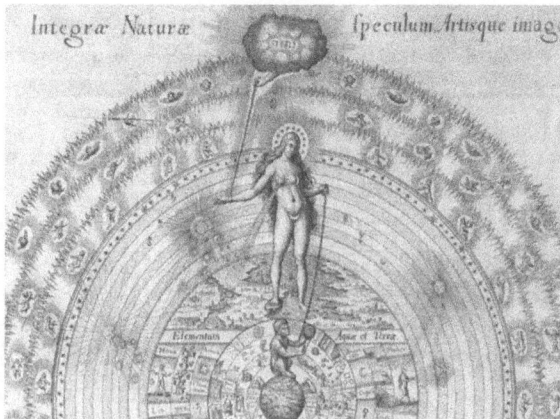

The Third Day

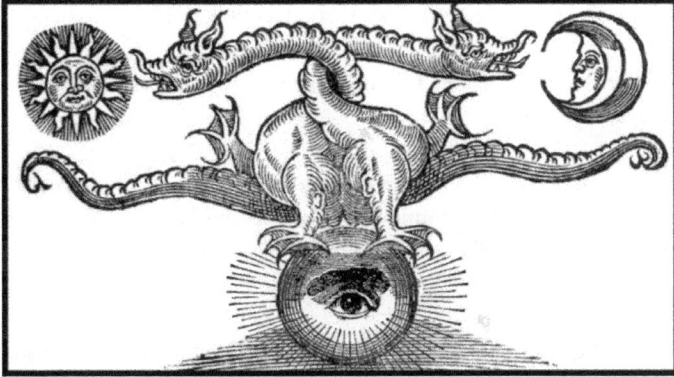

Now as soon as the lovely day was broken, and the bright Sun, having raised himself above the hills, had again took himself to his appointed office in the high Heaven, my good champions began to rise out of their beds, and leisurely to make themselves ready for the Inquisition. Whereupon, one after another, they came again into the hall, and saying good morning, demanded how we had slept that night; and having seen our bonds, there were some that reproved us for being so cowardly, and because we had not, rather, like them, hazarded upon all adventures. However, some of them whose hearts still smote them made no loud cry of the business. We excused ourselves with our ignorance, hoping we should now soon be set at liberty, and learn wisdom by this disgrace, that they on the contrary had not yet altogether escaped; and perhaps their greatest danger was still to come.

At length everyone being assembled again, the trumpets began again to sound and the kettle drums to beat as formerly, and we then imagined nothing other but that the Bridegroom was ready to present himself; which nevertheless was a huge mistake. For it was again the Virgin of yesterday, who had arrayed herself all in red velvet, and girded herself with a white scarf. On her head she had a green wreath of laurel, which greatly suited her. Her train was now no more of small tapers, but consisted of two hundred men in armor, who were all (like her) clothed in red and white.

Now as soon as they were alighted from the throne, she came straight to us prisoners, and after she had saluted us, she said in few words:

"That some of you have been aware of your wretched condition is hugely pleasing to my most mighty Lord, and he is also resolved you shall fare the better for it."

And having seen me in my habit, she laughed and said,

"Goodness! Have you also submitted yourself to the yoke? I imagined you would have made yourself very smug."

With which words she caused my eyes to run over. After which she commanded that we should be unbound, and coupled together and placed in a station where we might easily see the Scales. For, she said, it may yet fare better with them, than with the presumptuous who still stand here at liberty.

Meanwhile the scales, which were entirely of gold, were hung up in the middle of the hall; there was also a little table covered with red velvet, and seven weights placed on it. First of all there was a pretty big one, next four little ones, lastly two great ones. And these weights were so heavy in proportion to their bulk, that no man can believe or comprehend it. But each of the armored men had, together with a naked sword, a strong rope; these she distributed according to the number of weights into seven bands, and out of every band chose one for their own weight; and then again sprang up into her high throne. Now as soon as she had made her reverence, in a very shrill tone she began to speak as follows:

> *Whoever goes into an artist's room*
> *And nothing knows of painting*
> *And yet will speak with much display*
> *Will yet be mocked by everyone.*
> *And he who enters artist's orders*
> *Who had not been selected*
> *And begins to paint with much display*
> *Will yet be mocked by everyone.*
> *And who will to a wedding come*
> *And had not bidden been,*
> *And yet does come with much display*
> *Will yet be mocked by everyone.*
> *And who will climb upon these scales*
> *And find he weighed not,*
> *But is shot up with mighty crash*
> *Will yet be mocked by everyone.*

As soon as the Virgin had finished speaking, one of the pages commanded each one to place himself according to his order, and one after another to step in. Which one of the Emperors made no scruple of, but first of all bowed himself a little towards the Virgin, and afterwards in all his stately attire went up: whereupon each Captain put in his weight, against which (to the wonder of all) he held out. But the last was too heavy for him, so that he must go forth; and that he did with so much anguish that (as it seemed to me) the Virgin herself had pity on him, and beckoned to her people to hold their peace; yet the good Emperor was bound and delivered over to the Sixth Band. Next after him again there came another Emperor, who stepped haughtily into the Scale, and, having a great thick book under his gown, he imagined he would not fail; but he was scarcely able to abide the third weight, and was unmercifully flung down, and his book in that upheaval fell from him, and all the soldiers began to laugh, and he was delivered up bound to the Third Band. Thus, it went also with some of the other Emperors, who were all shamefully laughed at and put in captivity.

After these there came forth a short little man with a curled brown beard, also an Emperor, who after the usual reverence got up, and held out so steadfastly, that I thought that had there been more weights ready he would have outstood them. To him the Virgin immediately arose, and bowed before him, making him put on a gown of red velvet, and finally gave him a branch of laurel, of which she had a good store upon her throne, upon the steps of which she asked him to sit down. Now how it fared with the rest of the Emperors, Kings and Lords after him, would take too long to recount; but I cannot leave unmentioned that few of those great personages held out. However, various eminent virtues (beyond my hopes) were found in many. One could stand out this, the second another, some two, some three, four or five, but few could attain to the just perfection; and everyone who failed was miserably laughed at by the bands.

After the Inquisition had also passed over the gentry, the learned, and unlearned, and all the rest, and in each condition perhaps one, it may be two, but for the most part none, was found perfect, it came at length to those honest gentlemen the vagabond cheaters, and rascally *Lapidem Spitalanficum* makers, who were set upon the Scale with such scorn that I myself, in spite of all my grief, was ready to burst my belly with laughing, nor could the very prisoners themselves refrain. For the most part could not abide that severe trial, but were jerked out of the Scale with whips and scourges, and led to the other prisoners, but to a suitable band. Thus, of so great a throng so few remained, that I am ashamed to reveal their number. However, there were persons of quality also amongst them, who notwithstanding were (like the rest) honored with velvet robes and wreaths of laurel.

45

The Inquisition being completely finished, and none but we poor coupled hounds standing aside, at length one of the Captains stepped forth, and said,

"Gracious Madam, if it please your Ladyship, let these poor men who acknowledged their misunderstanding be set upon the Scale too, without their incurring any danger of penalty, and only for recreation's sake, if perhaps anything that is right may be found amongst them."

In the first place I was in great perplexity, for in my anguish this was my only comfort, that I was not to stand in such ignominy, or to be lashed out of the Scale. For I did not doubt that many of the prisoners wished that they had stayed ten nights with us in the hall. Yet since the Virgin consented, so it must be, and we were untied and one after another set up. Now although the most part miscarried, they were neither laughed at, nor scourged, but peaceably placed on one side. My companion was the fifth, and he held out bravely, whereupon all, but especially the Captain who made the request for us, applauded him, and the Virgin showed him the usual respect. After him again two more were dispatched in an instant. But I was the eighth.

Now as soon as (with trembling) I stepped up, my companion who already sat by in his velvet looked friendlily upon me, and the Virgin herself smiled a little.

But for as much as I outstood all the weights, the Virgin commanded them to draw me up by force, wherefore three men also hung on the other side of the beam, and yet nothing could prevail. Whereupon one of the pages immediately stood up, and cried out exceedingly loud, *"THAT'S HE"*: upon which the other replied, *"Then let him gain his liberty;"* which the Virgin accorded. And, being received with due ceremonies, the choice was given me to release one of the captives, whosoever I pleased; whereupon I made no long deliberation, but elected the first Emperor whom I had long pitied, who was immediately set free, and with all respect seated amongst us.

Now the last being set up, and the weights proving too heavy for him, in the meantime the Virgin had spotted my roses, which I had taken out of my hat into my hands, and thereupon presently through her page graciously requested them of me, and I readily sent them to her.

And so, this first Act was finished about ten in the morning. Whereupon the trumpets began to sound again, which nevertheless we could not as yet see.

Meantime the bands were to step aside with their prisoners and await the judgment. After which a council of the seven captains and us was set, and the business was propounded by the Virgin as President, who desired each one to give his opinion how the prisoners were to be dealt with. The first opinion was that they should all be put to death, yet one more severely than another, namely those who had presumptuously intruded themselves contrary to the express conditions. Others would have them kept close prisoners. Both of which pleased neither the President, nor me. At length by one of the Emperors (the same whom I had freed), my companion, and myself, the affair was brought to this point: that first of all the principal Lords should with a fitting respect be led out of the Castle; others might be carried out somewhat more scornfully. These would be stripped, and caused to run out naked; the fourth should be hunted out with rods, whips or dogs. Those who the day before willingly surrendered themselves, might be allowed to depart without any blame. And last of all those presumptuous ones, and they who behaved themselves so unseemly at dinner the day before, should be punished in body and life according to each man's demerit. This opinion pleased the Virgin well, and obtained the upper hand. There was moreover another dinner vouchsafed them, which they were soon told about. But the execution was deferred till twelve noon.

Herewith the Senate arose, and the Virgin also, together with her attendants, returned to her usual quarter. But the uppermost table in the room was allotted to us, they are requesting us to take it in good part until the business was fully dispatched. And then we should be conducted to the Lord Bridegroom and the Bride, with which we were at present well content. Meanwhile the prisoners were again brought into the hall, and each man seated according to his quality. They were likewise told to behave themselves somewhat more civilly than they had done the day before, about which they yet did not need to have been admonished, for without this, they had already put up their pipes.

And this I can boldly say, not with flattery, but in the love of truth, that commonly those persons who were of the highest rank best understood how to behave themselves in so unexpected a misfortune. Their treatment was but indifferent, yet respectful; neither could they yet see their attendants, but to us they were visible, at which I was exceedingly joyful. Now although Fortune had exalted us, yet we did not take upon us more than the rest, advising them to be of good cheer, the event would not be so bad. Now although they would gladly have us reveal their sentence, yet we were so deeply obligated that none of us dared open his mouth about it.

Nevertheless, we comforted them as well as we could, drinking with them to see if the wine might make them any more cheerful. Our table was covered with red velvet, beset with drinking cups of pure silver and gold, which the rest could not behold without amazement and very great anguish. But before we had seated ourselves, in came the two pages, presenting everyone on the Bridegroom's behalf with the Golden Fleece with a flying Lion, requesting us to wear them at the table, and as became us, to observe the reputation and dignity of the Order which his Majesty had now vouchsafed us; and we should be ratified with suitable ceremonies. This we received with profoundest submission, promising obediently to perform whatsoever his Majesty should please. Besides these, the noble page had a schedule in which we were set down in order. And for my part I should not otherwise wish to conceal my place, if perhaps it might not be interpreted as pride in me, which is expressly against the fourth weight.

Now because our entertainment was exceedingly stately, we demanded of one of the pages whether we might not have leave to send some choice bit to our friends and acquaintances; he made no difficulty of it, and everyone sent plentifully to his acquaintances by the waiters, although they saw none of them; and because they did not know where it came from, I myself wished to carry something to one of them. But as soon as I had risen, one of the waiters was at my elbow, saying he desired me to take friendly warning, for if one of the pages had seen it, it would have come to the King's ear, who would certainly have taken it amiss of me; but since none had observed it but himself, he did not intend to betray me, but that I ought for the time to come to have better regard for the dignity of the order. With which words the servant really astonished me so much that for a long time afterwards I scarcely moved in my seat, yet I returned him thanks for his faithful warning, as well as I was able in my haste and fear.

Soon after, the drums began to beat again, to which we were already accustomed: for we knew well it was the Virgin, so we prepared ourselves to receive her; she was now coming in with her usual train, upon her high seat, one of the pages bearing before her a very tall goblet of gold, and the other a patent in parchment. Having alighted from the seat in a marvelous skillful manner, she took the goblet from the page, and presented the same on the King's behalf, saying that it was brought from his Majesty, and that in honor of him we should cause it to go round. Upon the cover of this gob- let stood Fortune curiously cast in gold, who had in her hand a red flying ensign, because of which I drunk somewhat more sadly, having been all too well acquainted with Fortune's waywardness. But the Virgin as well as us was adorned with the Golden Fleece and Lion, from which I observed that perhaps she was the president of the Order. So, we asked of her how the Order might be named. She answered that it was not yet the right time to reveal this, till the affair with the prisoners was dispatched. And therefore, their eyes were still veiled; and what had hitherto happened to us, was to them only like an offence and scandal, although it was to be accounted as nothing in regard to the honor that attended us. Hereupon she began to distinguish the patent which the other page held into two different parts, out of which about this much was read before the first company:

"*That they should confess that they had too lightly given credit to false fictitious books, had assumed too much to themselves, and so come into this Castle, although they were never invited into it, and perhaps the most part had presented themselves with design to make their market here, and afterwards to live in greater pride and lordliness; and thus one had seduced another, and plunged him into this disgrace and ignominy, wherefore they were deservedly to be soundly punished.*"

Which they with great humility readily acknowledged, and gave their hands upon it. After which a severe check was given to the rest, much to this purpose:

"*That they very well knew, and were in their consciences convinced, that they had forged false fictitious books, had fooled others, and cheated them, and thereby had diminished regal dignity amongst all. They knew likewise what ungodly deceitful figures they had made use of, in so much as they spared not even the Divine Trinity, but accustomed themselves to cheat people all the country over. It was also now as clear as day with what practices they had endeavored to ensnare the true guests, and introduce the ignorant: in such a manner that it was manifest to all the world that they wallowed in open whoredom, adultery, gluttony, and other uncleanness: All which was against the express orders of our Kingdom. In brief, they knew they had disparaged Kingly Majesty, even amongst the common sort, and therefore they should confess themselves to be manifest convicted vagabond-cheaters, knaves and rascals, whereby they deserved to be kept from the company of civil people, and severely punished.*"

The good artists were loath to come to this confession, but inasmuch as not only the Virgin herself threatened them, and swore that they would die, but the other party also vehemently raged at them, and unanimously cried out that they had most wickedly seduced them out of the Light, they at length, to prevent a huge misfortune, confessed the same with sadness, and yet withal alleged that what had happened here was not to be animadverted upon them in the worst sense. For inasmuch as the Lords were absolutely resolved to get into the Castle, and had promised great sums of money to that effect, each one had used all craft to seize upon something, and so things were brought to that state that was now manifest before their eyes. But just because it had not succeeded, "*They*", in their opinion, "*had deserved no less than the Lords themselves; Who should have had so much understanding as to consider that, if anyone could be sure of getting in, he should not have clambered over the wall with them, that there should be so great peril for the sake of a slight gain?*"

Their books also sold so well, that whoever had no other means to maintain himself, had to engage in such a deception. They hoped moreover, that if a right judgment were made, they should be found in no way to have miscarried, for they had behaved themselves towards the Lords, as became Servants, upon their earnest entreaty.

But answer was made to them that his Royal Majesty had determined to punish them all, every man, although one more severely than another. For although what had been alleged by them was partly true, and therefore the Lords should not wholly be indulged, yet they had good reason to prepare themselves for death, they who had so presumptuously obtruded themselves, and perhaps seduced the more ignorant against their will; as likewise those who had violated Royal Majesty with false books, for the same might be shown from their very writings and books.

Hereupon many began to lament, cry, weep, entreat and prostrate themselves most piteously, all of which notwithstanding could avail them nothing, and I marveled much how the Virgin could be so resolute, when their misery caused our eyes to run over, and moved our compassion (although the most part of them had procured us much trouble and vexation). For she presently dispatched her page, who brought with him all the Cuirassiers who had this day been appointed at the Scales, who were each of them commanded to take his own to him, and in an orderly procession, so that each Cuirassier should go with one of the prisoners, to conduct them into her great garden. At which time each one so exactly recognized his own man, that I marveled at it. Leave was also likewise given to my companions of yesterday to go out into the garden unbound, and to be present at the execution of the sentence. Now as soon as every man had come forth, the Virgin mounted up into her high throne, requesting us to sit down upon the steps, and to appear at the judgment; which we did not refuse, but left everything standing upon the table (except the goblet, which the Virgin committed to the pages' keeping) and went forth in our robes, upon the throne, which moved by itself as gently as if we passed through the air, till in this manner we came into the garden, where we all arose together.

This garden was not extraordinarily curious, but it pleased me that the trees were planted in such good order. Besides, there ran in it a most costly fountain, adorned with wonderful figures and inscriptions and strange characters (which, God willing, I shall mention in a future book). In this garden was raised a wooden scaffold, hung about with curiously painted figured coverlets. Now there were four galleries made one over another; the first was more glorious than any of the rest, and therefore covered with a white taffeta curtain, so that at that time we could not perceive who was behind it. The second was empty and uncovered. Again, the last two were covered with red and blue taffeta. Now as soon as we had come to the scaffold, the Virgin bowed herself down to the ground, at which we were mightily terrified, for we could easily guess that the King and Queen must not be far off. Now we also having duly performed our reverence, the Virgin led us up by the winding stairs into the second gallery, where she placed herself uppermost, and us in our former order. But how the Emperor whom I had released behaved himself towards me, both at this time and also before at the table, I cannot well relate without slander of wicked tongues. For he might well have imagined in what anguish and solicitude he should now have been, in case he were at present to attend the judgment with such ignominy, and that only through me he had now attained such dignity and worthiness.

Meanwhile the Virgin who first of all brought me the invitation, and whom until now I had never since seen, came in. First she gave one blast upon her trumpet, and then with a very loud voice declared the sentence in this manner:

"The King's Majesty my most gracious Lord could wish with all his heart that each and every one here assembled had upon his Majesty's invitation presented themselves so qualified as that they might (to his honor) with greatest frequency have adorned this his appointed nuptial and joyful feast. But since it has otherwise pleased Almighty God, his Majesty has nothing about which to murmur, but must be forced, contrary to his own inclination, to abide by the ancient and laudable constitutions of this Kingdom. But now, so that his Majesty's innate clemency may be celebrated all over the world, he has so far absolutely dealt with his Council and estates, that the usual sentence shall be considerably lenified.

So in the first place he is willing to vouchsafe to the Lords and Potentates, not only their lives entirely, but also that he will freely and frankly dismiss them; friendlily and courteously entreating your Lordships not at all to take it in evil part that you cannot be present at his Majesty's Feast of Honor; but to remember that there is notwithstanding more imposed upon your Lordships by God Almighty (who in the distribution of his gifts has an incomprehensible consideration) than you can duly and easily sustain. Neither is your reputation hereby prejudiced, although you be rejected by this our Order, since we cannot all of us do all things at once. But for as much as your Lordships have been seduced by base rascals, it shall not, on their part, pass unrevenged. And furthermore, his Majesty resolves shortly to communicate to your Lordships a catalogue of heretics or Index Expurgatorius, that you may henceforth be able to discern between the good and the evil with better judgment. And because his Majesty before long also intends to rummage his library, and offer up the seductive writings to Vulcan, he friendlily, humbly, and courteously entreats every one of your Lordships to do the same with your own, whereby it is to be hoped that all evil and mischief may for the time to come be remedied. And you are withal to be admonished, never henceforth to covet an entrance here so inconsiderately, lest the former excuse about seducers be taken *from you, and you fall into disgrace and contempt with all men. Finally, for as much as the estates of the land still have something to demand of your Lordships, his Majesty hopes that no man will think much to redeem himself with a chain or whatever else he has about him, and so in friendly manner to depart from us, and through our safe conduct to take himself home again.*

The others who did not stand up to the first, third and fourth weight, his Majesty will not so lightly dismiss. But so that they also may now experience his Majesty's gentleness, it is his command to strip them stark naked and so send them forth.

Those who in the second and fifth weight were found too light, shall besides stripping, be noted with one, two or more brand-marks, according as each one was lighter or heavier.

They who were drawn up by the sixth or seventh, and not by the rest, shall be somewhat more graciously dealt with, and so forward. (For to every combination there was a certain punishment ordained, which is here too long to recount.)

They who yesterday separated themselves freely of their own accord, shall go out at liberty without any blame.

Finally, the convicted vagabond-cheaters who could move up none of the weights, shall as occasion serves be punished in body and life, with the sword, halter, water and rods. And such execution of judgment shall be inviolably observed as an example to others."

Herewith our Virgin broke her wand, and the other who read the sentence blew her trumpet, and stepped with most profound reverence towards those who stood behind the curtain.

But here I cannot omit to reveal something to the reader concerning the number of our prisoners, of whom those who weighed one, were seven; those who weighed two, were twenty-one; they who three, thirty-five; they who four, thirty-five; those who five, twenty-one; those who six, seven; but he that came to the seventh, and yet could not well raise it, he was only one, and indeed the same whom I released. Besides these, of them who wholly failed there were many; but of those who drew all the weights from the ground, but few. And as these each stood before us, so I diligently numbered them and noted them down in my table-book; and it is very admirable that amongst all those who weighed anything, none was equal to another. For although amongst those who weighed three, there were thirty-five, yet one of them weighed the first, second, and third, another the third, fourth, and fifth, a third, the fifth, sixth, and seventh, and so on. It is likewise very wonderful that amongst one hundred and twenty-six who weighed anything, none was equal to another; and I would very willingly name them all, with each man's weight, were it not as yet forbidden me. But I hope it may hereafter be published with the Interpretation.

Now this judgment being read over, the Lords in the first place were well satisfied, because in such severity they did not dare look for a mild sentence. So, they gave more than was desired of them, and each one redeemed himself with chains, jewels, gold, money and other things, as much as they had about them, and with reverence took leave. Now although the King's servants were forbidden to jeer at any at his going away, yet some unlucky birds could not hold their laughter, and certainly it was sufficiently ridiculous to see them pack away with such speed, without once looking behind them. Some desired that the promised catalogue might at once be dispatched after them, and then they would take such order with their books as should be pleasing to his Majesty; which was again assured. At the door was given to each of them out of a cup a draught of FORGETFULNESS, so that he might have no further memory of misfortune.

After these the Volunteers departed, who because of their ingenuity were allowed to pass, but yet so as never to return again in the same fashion. But if to them (as likewise to the others) anything further were revealed, then they should be welcome guests.

Meanwhile others were stripping, in which also an inequality (according to each man's demerit) was observed. Some were sent away naked, without other hurt. Others were driven out with small bells. Some were scourged forth. In brief the punishments were so various, that I am not able to recount them all. In the end it came to the last, with whom a somewhat longer time was spent, for while some were being hung, some beheaded, some forced to leap into the water, and the rest otherwise being dispatched, much time was consumed. Verily at this execution my eyes ran over, not indeed in regard of the punishment, which they for their impudence well deserved, but in contemplation of human blindness, in that we are continually busying ourselves in that which ever since the first Fall has been hitherto sealed up to us. Thus, the garden which so recently was quite full, was soon emptied, so that besides the soldiers there was not a man left.

Now as soon as this was done, and silence had been kept for the space of five minutes, there came forth a beautiful snow-white unicorn with a golden collar (having on it certain letters) about his neck. In the same place he bowed himself down upon both his forefeet, as if hereby he had shown honor to the lion, who stood so immovably upon the fountain, that I had taken him to be of stone or brass. The lion immediately took the naked sword which he had in his paw, and broke it in two in the middle, and the pieces of it, it seemed to me, sunk into the fountain;

after which he roared for so long, until a white dove brought a branch of olive in her bill, which the lion devoured in an instant, and so was quieted. And so, the unicorn returned to his place with joy.

Hereupon our Virgin led us down again by the winding stairs from the scaffold, and so we again made our reverence towards the curtain. We were to wash our hands and heads in the fountain, and there to wait a little while in our order, till the King was again returned into his hall through a certain secret gallery, and then we were also conducted into our former lodging with choice music, pomp, state, and pleasant discourse. And this was done about four in the afternoon.

But so that in the meantime the time might not seem too long to us, the Virgin bestowed on each of us a noble page, who were not only richly dressed, but also exceedingly learned, so that they could so aptly discourse upon all subjects that we had good reason to be ashamed of ourselves. These were commanded to lead us up and down the Castle, but only into certain places, and if possible, to shorten the time according to our desire. Meanwhile the Virgin took leave with this consolation, that at supper she would be with us again, and after that celebrate the ceremonies of the hanging up of the weights, requesting that we would in patience wait till the next day, for on the morrow we must be presented to the King.

She having thus departed from us, each of us did what best pleased him. One part viewed the excellent paintings, which they copied out for themselves, and considered also what the wonderful characters might signify. Others wanted to occupy themselves again with meat and drink.

I caused my page to conduct me (together with my companion) up and down the Castle, which walk I shall never regret as long as I have a day to live. For besides many other glorious antiquities, the Royal Sepulcher was also showed to me, by which I learned more than is extant in all books. There in the same place stands also the glorious phoenix (about which, two years ago, I published a particular small discourse). And I am resolved (in case this narration shall prove useful) to set forth several particular treatises concerning the lion, eagle, griffin, falcon and the like, together with their draughts and inscriptions. It grieves me for my other companions, that they neglected such precious treasures. And yet I cannot but think it was the special will of God that it should be so. I indeed reaped the most benefit from my page, for according as each one's genius lay, so he led whoever was entrusted to him into the quarters and places which were pleasing to him. Now the keys belonging hereunto were committed to my page, and therefore this good fortune happened to me before the rest; for although he invited others to come in, yet they imagining such tombs to be only in the churchyard, thought they should get there well enough, whenever anything was to be seen there. Neither shall these monuments (as both of us copied and transcribed them) be withheld from my thankful scholars.

The other thing that was shown to us two was the noble library as it was all together before the Reformation. Of which (although it makes my heart rejoice as often as I call it to mind) I have so much the less to say, because the catalogue of it is very shortly to be published. At the entry to this room stands a great book, the like of which I never saw, in which all the figures, rooms, portals, also all the writings, riddles and the like, to be seen in the whole Castle, are delineated. Now although we made a promise concerning this also, yet at present I must contain myself, and first learn to know the world better. In every book stands its author painted; of which (as I understood) many were to be burnt, so that even their memory might be blotted out from amongst the righteous.

Now having taken a full view of this, and having scarcely gone forth, another page came running to us, and having whispered something in our page's ear, he delivered up the keys to him, who immediately carried them up the winding stairs. But our page was very much out of countenance, and we having set hard upon him with entreaties, he declared to us that the King's Majesty would by no means permit that either of the two, namely the library and sepulchers, should be seen by any man, and therefore he besought us as we cared for his life, to reveal this to no man, he having already utterly denied it. Whereupon both of us stood hovering between joy and fear, yet it continued in silence, and no man-made further enquiry about it. Thus, in both places we passed three hours, which I do not at all repent.

Now although it had already struck seven, yet nothing had so far been given us to eat; however, our hunger was easy to abate by constant reviving, and I could be well content to fast all my life long with such entertainment. About this time the curious fountains, mines, and all kinds of art-shops, were also shown to us, of which there was none but surpassed all our arts, even if they should all be melted into one mass. All their chambers were built in a semi-circle, so that they might have before their eyes the costly clockwork which was erected upon a fair turret in the centre, and regulate themselves according to the course of the planets, which were to be seen on it in a glorious manner. And hence I could easily conjecture where our artists failed; however, it's none of my duty to inform them.

At length I came into a spacious room (shown indeed to the rest a great while before) in the middle of which stood a terrestrial globe, whose diameter was thirty feet, although nearly half of it, except a little which was covered with the steps, was let into the earth. Two men might readily turn this globe about with all its furniture, so that no more of it was ever to be seen, just so much as was above the horizon. Now although I could easily conceive that this was of some special use, yet I could not understand what those ringlets of gold (which were upon it in several places) served for; at which my page laughed, and advised me to view them more closely. In brief, I found there my native country noted in gold also; whereupon my companion sought his, and found that so too.

Now for as much as the same happened in a similar way to the rest who stood by, the page told us for certain that it was yesterday declared to the King's Majesty by their old Atlas (so is the Astronomer named) that all the gilded points exactly answered to their native countries, according as had been shown to each of them. And therefore he also, as soon as he perceived that I undervalued myself and that nevertheless there stood a point upon my native country, moved one of the Captains to entreat for us that we should be set upon the scale (without peril) at all adventures; especially seeing one of our native countries had a notable good mark. And truly it was not without reason that he, the page who had the greatest power of all the rest, was bestowed on me. For this I then returned him thanks, and immediately looked more diligently upon my native country, and found moreover that besides the ringlet, there were also certain delicate streaks upon it, which nevertheless I would not be thought to speak about to my own praise and glory.

I saw much more too upon this globe than I am willing to reveal. Let each man take into consideration why every city does not produce a philosopher. After this he led us right into the globe, which was thus made: on the sea (there being a large square beside it) was a tablet, on which stood three dedications and the author's name, which a man might gently lift up and by a little joined board go into the centre, which was capable of holding four persons, being nothing but a round board on which we could sit, and at ease, by broad daylight (it was now already dark) contemplate the stars. To my thinking they were mere carbuncles which glittered in an agreeable order, and moved so gallantly that I had scarcely any mind ever to go out again, as the page afterwards told the Virgin, with which she often teased me. For it was already supper-time, and I had so much amused myself in the globe, that I was almost the last at the table; so I made no more delay, but having put on my gown again (which I had before laid aside) and stepping to the table, the waiters treated me with so much reverence and honor, that for shame I dared not look up, and so unawares permitted the Virgin, who attended me on one side, to stand, which she soon perceiving, twitched me by the gown, and so led me to the table. To speak any further concerning the music, or the rest of that magnificent entertainment, I hold it needless, both because it is not possible to express it well enough, and because I have reported it above according to my power. In brief, there was nothing there but art and amenity.

Now after we had related our employment since noon to each other (however, not a word was spoken of the library and monuments), being already merry with the wine, the Virgin began thus:

"My Lords, I have a great contention with one of my sisters. In our chamber we have an eagle. Now we cherish him with such diligence, that each of us is desirous to be the best beloved, and upon that score we have many a squabble. One day we concluded to go both together to him, and toward whom he should show himself most friendly, hers should he properly be. This we need, and I (as commonly) carried in my hand a branch of laurel, but my sister had none. Now as soon as he saw us both, he immediately gave my sister another branch which he had in his beak, and reached for mine, which I gave him.

Now each of us hereupon imagined herself to be best beloved of him; which way am I to resolve myself? "

This modest proposal of the Virgin pleased us all mighty well, and each one would gladly have heard the solution, but inasmuch as they all looked to me, and wanted me to begin, my mind was so extremely confounded that I knew not what else to do with it but propound another in its stead, and therefore said:

"Gracious Lady, your Ladyship's question would easily be resolved if one thing did not perplex me. I had two companions, both of which loved me exceedingly; now they are being doubtful which of them was most dear to me, concluded to run to me, I unawares, and that he whom I should then embrace should be the right. This they did, yet one of them could not keep pace with the other, so he stayed behind and wept, the other I embraced with amazement. Now when they had afterwards discovered the business to me, I did not know how to resolve myself, and have since then let it rest in this manner, until I may find some good advice herein."

The Virgin wondered at it, and well observed where-about I was, where-upon she replied,

"Well then, let us both be quit;"

and then desired the solution from the rest.
But I had already made them wise. So, the next began thus.

"In the city where I live, a Virgin was recently condemned to death, but the Judge, being somewhat pitiful towards her, caused it to be proclaimed that if any man desired to

become the Virgin's Champion, he should have free leave to do it. Now she had two lovers; the one presently made himself ready, and came into the lists to await his adversary; afterwards the other also presented himself, but coming somewhat too late, he resolved nevertheless to fight, and willingly suffer himself to be vanquished, so that the Virgin's life might be preserved, which also succeeded accordingly."

Whereupon each challenged her:

"Now my Lords, instruct me, to which of them of right does she belong?"

The Virgin could hold out no longer and said,

"I thought to have gained much information, and have got myself into the net, but yet would gladly hear whether there are any more to come."

"Yes, that there are," answered the third, *"a stranger adventure has not yet been recounted than that which happened to me. In my youth I loved a worthy maid: now so that my love might attain its desired end, I used to employ an ancient matron, who easily brought me to her. Now it happened that the maid's brethren came in upon us just as we three were together, and were in such a rage that they would have taken my life, but upon my vehement supplication, they at length forced me to swear to take each of them for a year, to be my wedded wife. Now tell me, my Lords, should I take the old, or the young one first?"*

We all laughed sufficiently at this riddle, and though some of them muttered to one another about it, yet none would undertake to unfold it.

Hereupon the fourth began:

"In a certain city there dwelt an honorable lady, who was beloved of all, but especially by a young nobleman, who was too importunate with her. At length she gave him this determination, that if he could lead her into a fair green garden of roses in a cold winter, then he should obtain what he desired, but if not, he must resolve never to see her again. The nobleman traveled to all countries to find such a man as might perform this, till at length he found a little old man that promised to do it for him, if he would assure him of half his estate; which he having consented to the other, was as good as his word. Whereupon he invited the aforesaid lady to his garden, where, contrary to her expectation, she found all things green, pleasant and warm, and remembering her promise, she only requested that she might once more return to her lord, to whom with sighs and tears she bewailed her lamentable condition. But because he sufficiently perceived her faithfulness, he dispatched her back to her lover who had so dearly purchased her, so that she might give him satisfaction. This husband's integrity did so mightily affect the nobleman, that he thought it a sin to touch so honest a wife; so, he

sent her home again with honor to her lord. Now the little man perceiving such faith in both these, would not, however poor he was, be the least in honor, but restored to the nobleman all his goods again and went his way. Now, my lords, I know not which of these persons may have shown the greatest ingenuity?"

Here our tongues were quite cut off. Neither would the Virgin make any other reply, but only that another should go on.

So, the fifth, without delay, began:

"My Lords, I do not wish to make long work of this; who has the greater joy, he that beholds what he loves, or he that only thinks on it?"

"He that beholds it." said the Virgin.

"No." I answered.

Hereupon a debate arose, so the sixth called out,

"My lords, I am to take a wife; now I have before me a maid, a married wife, and a widow; ease me of this doubt, and I will afterwards help to order the rest."

"It goes well there," replied the seventh, *"where a man has a choice, but with me the case is otherwise. In my youth I loved a fair and virtuous virgin from the bottom of my heart, and she loved me in similar manner; however, because of her friends' denial we could not come together in wedlock. Whereupon she was married to another, yet an honest and discreet person, who maintained her honorably and with affection, until she came to the pains of childbirth, which went so hard for her that all thought she was dead, so with much state and great mourning she was interred. Now I thought to myself, during her life you could have no part in this woman, but now she is dead you may embrace and kiss her sufficiently; so, I took my servant with me, who dug her up by night. Now having opened the coffin and locked her in my arms, feeling about her heart, I found some little motion in it still, which increased more and more from my warmth, till at last I perceived that she was indeed still alive. So, I quietly bore her home, and after I had warmed her chilled body with a costly bath of herbs, I committed her to my mother until she brought forth a fair son, whom I caused to be nursed faithfully, as for his mother. After two days (she being then in great amazement) I revealed to her all the preceding affair, requesting her for the time to come to live with me as a wife; against which she found exception, in case it should be grievous to her husband who had maintained her well and honorably. But if it could be otherwise, she was obliged in love at present to one as well as the other. Now after two months (being then about to make a journey elsewhere) I invited her husband as a guest, and amongst other things demanded of*

him whether, if his deceased wife should come home again, he would be content to receive her. He affirmed it with tears and lamentations, and I brought him his wife together with his son, and gave an account of all the preceding business, entreating him to ratify with his consent my intended espousals. After a long dispute he could not deny me my right, but had to leave me his wife. But there was still a debate about the son."

Here the Virgin interrupted him, and said,

"It makes me wonder how you could double the afflicted man's grief."

"What?" he answered, *"Was I not concerned about it?"*

Upon this there arose a dispute amongst us, yet most affirmed that he had acted correctly.

"No," he said, *"I freely returned him both his wife and his son. Now tell me, my Lords, was my honesty, or this man's joy, the greater?"*

These words had so much cheered the Virgin that (as if it had been for the sake of these two) she caused a health to be drunk.

After which the rest of the proposals went on somewhat perplexedly, so that I could not retain them all; yet this comes to my mind, that one said that a few years before he had seen a physician, who brought a parcel of wood against winter, with which he warmed himself all winter long; but as soon as the spring returned he sold the very same wood again, and so had use of it for nothing.

"Here there must be skill," said the Virgin, *"but the time is now past."*

"Yes," replied my companion, *"whoever does not understand how to resolve all the riddles may give each man notice of it by a proper messenger, and he will not be denied."*

At this time, they began to say grace, and we arose all together from the table, satisfied and merry rather than satiated; and it is to be wished that all invitations and feastings were kept like this. Having now taken a few turns up and down the hall again, the Virgin asked us whether we desired to begin the wedding.

"Yes, noble and virtuous lady." said one. Whereupon she privately dispatched a page, and yet in the meantime proceeded in discourse with us. In brief she had already become so familiar with us, that I ventured to request her Name. The Virgin smiled at my curiosity, yet was not moved, but replied:

"My Name contains five and fifty, and yet has only eight letters; the third is the third part of the fifth, which added to the sixth will produce a number whose root shall exceed the third itself by just the first, and it is the half of the fourth. Now the fifth and the seventh are equal, the last and the fifth are also equal, and make with the second as much as the sixth, which contains just four more than the third tripled. Now tell me, my lord, what am I called?"

The answer was intricate enough to me, yet I did not leave off, but said,

"Noble and virtuous lady, may I not have only one letter?"

"Yes," she said, *"that may well be done."*
"What then," I replied again, *"may the seventh contain?"*

"It contains," she said, *"as many as there are lords here."*

With this I was content, and easily found her Name, at which she was very pleased, and assured us that much more should yet be revealed to us.

Meantime certain virgins had made themselves ready, and came in with great ceremony. First of all two youths carried lights before them; one of them was of jocund countenance, sprightly eyes and gentle proportion. The other looked rather angry, and whatever he would have, must be, as I afterwards perceived.

After them first followed four virgins. One looked shame-facedly towards the earth, very humble in behavior. The second also was a modest, bashful virgin.

The third, as she entered the room, seemed amazed at something, and as I understood, she cannot easily abide where there is too much mirth. The fourth brought with her certain small wreaths, thereby to manifest her kindness and liberality.

After these four came two who were somewhat more gloriously appareled; they saluted us courteously. One of them had a gown of sky color spangled with golden stars. The other's was green, beautified with red and white stripes. On their heads they had thin flying tiffanies, which adorned them most becomingly.

At last came one on her own, who had a coronet on her head, but looked up rather towards heaven than towards earth. We all thought it was the Bride, but were much mistaken, although otherwise in honor, riches and state she much surpassed the Bride; and she afterwards ruled the whole Wedding. Now on this occasion we all followed our Virgin, and fell down on our knees; however, she showed herself to be extremely humble, offering everyone her hand, and admonishing us not to be too much surprised at this, for this was one of her smallest bounties; but to lift up our eyes to our Creator, and learn hereby to acknowledge his all-power, and so proceed in our enterprising course, employing this grace to the praise of God, and the good of man. In sum, her words were quite different from those of our Virgin, who was somewhat more worldly. They pierced me through even to my bones and marrow.

"And you," she said further to me, *"have received more than others, see that you also make a larger return."*

This to me was a very strange sermon; for as soon as we saw the virgins with the music, we imagined we must soon begin to dance, but that time was not as yet come. Now the weights, which have been mentioned before, stood still in the same place, so the Duchess (I knew not yet who she was) commanded each virgin to take up one, but to our Virgin she gave her own, which was the last and greatest, and commanded us to follow behind. Our majesty was then somewhat abated, for I observed well that our Virgin was too good for us, and we were not so highly reputed as we ourselves were almost in part willing to fantasize. So, we went behind in our order, and were brought into the first chamber, where our Virgin in the first place hung up the Duchess' weight, during which an excellent spiritual hymn was sung. There was nothing costly in this room save only curious little prayer books which should never be missing.

In the middle was erected a pulpit, very convenient for prayer, in which the Duchess kneeled down, and about her we all had to kneel and pray after the Virgin, who read out of a book, that this Wedding might tend to the honor of God, and our own benefit. Afterwards we came into the second chamber, where the first Virgin hung up her weight too, and so forward until all the ceremonies were finished. Hereupon the Duchess again presented her hand to everyone, and departed hence with her virgin.

Our president stayed yet a while with us. But because it had already been night for two hours, she would no longer detain us. I thought she was glad of our company, yet she bade us good night, and wished us quiet rest, and so departed friendlily, although unwillingly, from us. Our pages were well instructed in their business, and therefore showed every man his chamber, and stayed with us too in another bed, so that in case we wanted anything we might make use of them. My chamber (of the rest I am not able to speak) was royally furnished with rare tapestries, and hung about with paintings. But above all things I delighted in my page, who was so excellently spoken, and experienced in the arts, that he spent yet another hour with me, and it was half past three when I first fell asleep. And this was the first night that I slept in quiet, and yet a scurvy dream would not let me rest; for all the night I was troubled with a door which I could not get open, but at last I did it. With these fantasies I passed the time, till at length towards day I awakened.

The Fourth Day

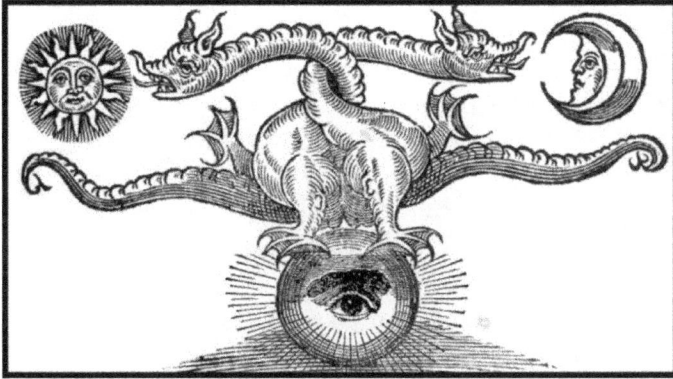

I was still lying in my bed, and leisurely surveying all the noble images and figures up and down about my chamber, when suddenly I heard the music of coronets, as if they were already in procession. My page jumped out of the bed as if he had been at his wit's end, and looked more like one dead than living. In what state I was then is easily imaginable, for he said,

"The rest are already presented to the King."

I did not know what else to do but weep outright and curse my own tardiness; yet I dressed myself, but my page was ready long before me, and ran out of the chamber to see how affairs might yet stand. But he soon returned, and brought with him this joyful news, that indeed the time was not yet, but I had only overslept my breakfast, they being unwilling to awaken me because of my age.

But now it was time for me to go with him to the fountain where most of them were assembled. With this consolation my spirit returned, so I was soon ready with my habit, and went after the page to the fountain in the garden, where I found that the lion, instead of his sword, had a pretty large tablet by him. Now having looked well at it, I found that it was taken out of the ancient monuments, and placed here for some special honor. The inscription was somewhat worn out with age, and therefore I have a mind to set it down here, as it is, and give everyone leave to consider it.

HERMES PRINCEPS.
POST TOT ILLATA
GENERI HUMANO DAMNA,
DEI CONSILIO:
ARTISQUE ADMINICULO,
MEDICINA SALUBRIS FACTUR
HEIC FLUO
Bibat ex me qui potest: lavet, qui vult: turbet qui audet:
BIBITE FRATRES, ET VIVITE

"Hermes the Prince. After many wounds inflicted on humankind, here by God's counsel and the help of the Art flow I, a healing medicine. Let him drink me who can: let him wash who will: let him trouble me who dare drink, brethren and live."

This writing might well be read and understood, and may therefore suitably be placed here, because it is easier than any of the rest.

Now after we had first washed ourselves out of the fountain, and every man had taken a draught out of an entirely golden cup, we were once again to follow the Virgin into the hall, and there put on new apparel, which was all of cloth of gold gloriously set out with flowers. There was also given to everyone another Golden Fleece, which was set about with precious stones, and various workmanship according to the utmost skill of each artificer. On it hung a weighty medal of gold, on which were figured the sun and moon in opposition; but on the other side stood this saying,

"The light of the moon shall be as the light of the sun, and the light of the sun shall be seven times lighter than at present."

But our former jewels were laid in a little casket, and committed to one of the waiters. After this the Virgin led us out in our order, where the musicians waited ready at the door, all appareled in red velvet with white guards. After which a door (which I never saw open before) to the Royal winding stairs was unlocked. There the Virgin led us, together with the music, up three hundred and sixty-five stairs; there we saw nothing that was not of extremely costly workmanship, full of artifice; and the further we went, the more glorious still was the furniture, until at length at the top we came under a painted arch, where the sixty virgins attended us, all richly appareled. Now as soon as they had bowed to us, and we, as well as we could, had returned our reverence, our musicians were sent away, and must go down the stairs again, the door being shut after them. After this a little bell was tolled; then in came in a beautiful Virgin who brought everyone a wreath of laurel. But our virgins had branches given them.

Meanwhile a curtain was drawn up, where I saw the King and Queen as they sat there in their majesty, and had not the Duchess yesterday so faithfully warned me, I should have forgotten myself, and have equaled this unspeakable glory to Heaven. For apart from the fact that the room glistened with gold and precious stones, the Queen's robes were moreover made so that I was not able to behold them. And whereas before I esteemed anything to be handsome, here all things so much surpassed the rest, as the stars in heaven are elevated.

In the meantime the Virgin came in, and so each of the virgins taking one of us by the hand, with most profound reverence presented us to the King, whereupon the Virgin began to speak thus:

"That to honor your Royal Majesties (most gracious King and Queen) these lords here present have ventured here in peril of body and life, your Majesties have reason to rejoice, especially since the greatest part are qualified for the enlarging of your Majesties' Estates and Empire, as you will find by a most gracious and particular examination of each of them. Herewith I desired to have them presented in humility to your Majesties, with most humble suit to discharge myself of this commission of mine, and most graciously to take sufficient information from each of them, concerning both my actions and omissions."

Hereupon she laid down her branch upon the ground. Now it would have been very fitting for one of us to have put in and said something on this occasion, but seeing we were all tongue-tied, at length the old Atlas stepped forward and spoke on the King's behalf:

"Their Royal Majesties do most graciously rejoice at your arrival, and wish that their Royal Grace be assured to all, and every man. And with your administration, gentle Virgin, they are most graciously satisfied, and accordingly a Royal Reward shall therefore be provided for you. Yet it is still their intention that you shall also continue to be with them this day, inasmuch as they have no reason to mistrust you."

Hereupon the Virgin humbly took up the branch again. And so, we for the first time were to step aside with our Virgin. This room was square on the front, five times broader than it was long; but towards the West it had a great arch like a porch, wherein in a circle stood three glorious royal thrones, yet the middlemost was somewhat higher than the rest. Now in each throne sat two persons. In the first sat a very ancient King with a grey beard, yet his consort was extraordinarily fair and young. In the third throne sat a black King of middle age, and by him a dainty old matron, not crowned, but covered with a veil. But in the middle sat the two young persons, and though they had likewise wreaths of laurel upon their heads, yet over them hung a large and costly crown. Now although they were not at this time so far as I had before imagined to myself, yet so it was to be. Behind them on a round form sat for the most part ancient men, yet none of them had any sword or other weapon about him, at which I wondered. Neither saw I any other bodyguard, but certain Virgins who were with us the day before, who sat on the sides of the arch.

Here I cannot pass over in silence how the little Cupid flew to and fro there, but for the most part he hovered over and played the wanton about the great crown; sometimes he seated himself between the two lovers, somewhat smiling upon them with his bow. Indeed, sometimes he made as if he would shoot one of us. In brief, this knave was so full of his waggery, that we would not even spare the little birds which flew in multitudes up and down the room, but tormented them all he could. The virgins also had their pastimes with him, but whenever they could catch him, it was not so easy a matter for him to get from them again. Thus, this little knave made all the sport and mirth.

Before the Queen stood a small but inexpressibly curious altar, on which lay a book covered with black velvet, a little overlaid with gold. By this stood a small taper in an ivory candlestick. Now although it was very small, yet it burnt continually, and was such that had not Cupid, in sport, now and then puffed upon it, we could not have conceived it to be fire. By this stood a sphere or celestial globe, which turned clearly about by itself. Next to this, a small striking-watch, and by that was a little crystal pipe or siphon-fountain, out of which perpetually ran a clear blood-red liquor. And last of all there was a skull, or death's head; in this was a white serpent, who was of such a length that though she wound about the rest of it in a circle, her tail still remained in one of the eyeholes until her head again entered the other; so she never stirred from her skull, unless it happened that Cupid twitched a little at her, for then she slipped in so suddenly that we all could not choose but marvel at it.

Together with this altar, there were up and down the room wonderful images, which moved themselves as if they had been alive, and had so strange a contrivance that it would be impossible for me to relate it all. Likewise, as we were passing out, there began such a marvelous kind of vocal music, that I could not tell for sure whether it was performed by the virgins who still stayed behind, or by the images themselves. Now we being satisfied for the time being, went away with our virgins, who (the musicians being already present) led us down the winding stairs again, and the door was diligently locked and bolted. As soon as we had come again into the hall, one of the virgins began:

"I wonder, Sister, that you dare hazard yourself amongst so many people."

"My Sister," replied our president, *"I am afraid of none so much as of this man,"* pointing at me."

This speech went to my heart, for I well understood that she mocked at my age, and indeed I was the oldest of them all. Yet she comforted me again with the promise that if I behaved myself well towards her, she would easily rid me of this burden.

Meantime a light meal was again brought in, and everyone's Virgin seated by him; they knew well how to shorten the time with handsome discourses, but what their discourses and sports were I dare not blab out of school. But most of the questions were about the arts, whereby I could easily gather that both young and old were conversant in knowledge. But still it ran in my thoughts how I might become young again, whereupon I was somewhat sadder.

The Virgin perceived this, and therefore began,

"I bet anything, if I lie with him tonight, he shall be pleasanter in the morning."

Hereupon they all began to laugh, and although I blushed all over, yet I had to laugh too at my own ill-luck.

Now there was one there who had a mind to return my disgrace upon the Virgin again, so he said,

"I hope not only we, but the virgins themselves too, will bear witness on behalf of our brother, that our lady president has promised to be his bedfellow tonight."

"I should be well content with it," replied the Virgin, *"if I had no reason to be afraid of my sisters here; there would be no hold with them should I choose the best and handsomest for myself, against their will."*

"My Sister," began another, *"we find by this that your high office doesn't make you proud; so if with your permission we might divide by lot the lords here present among us for bedfellows, you should with our good will have such a prerogative."*

We let this pass for a jest, and again began to discourse together. But our

Virgin could not leave tormenting us, and therefore began again.

"My lords, what about if we should let fortune decide which of us must lie together tonight?"

"Well," I said, "if it may not be otherwise, we cannot refuse such an offer." Now because it was concluded to make this trial after the meal, we resolved to sit no longer at table, so we arose, and each one walked up and down with his Virgin.

"No," said the Virgin, "it shall not be so yet, but let us see how fortune will couple us," upon which we were separated.

But now first arose a dispute how the business should be carried out; but this was only a premeditated device, for the Virgin instantly made the proposal that we should mix ourselves together in a ring, and that she beginning to count the seventh from herself, was to be content with the following seventh, whether it were a virgin, or a man. For our parts we were not aware of any craft, and therefore permitted it to be so; but when we thought we had mingled ourselves very well, the virgins nevertheless were so clever that each one knew her station beforehand. The Virgin began to reckon; the seventh from her was another virgin, the third seventh a virgin likewise, and this happened so long till (to our amazement) all the virgins came forth, and none of us was hit. Thus, we poor pitiful wretches remained standing alone, and were moreover forced to suffer ourselves to be jeered at, and to confess we were very handsomely tricked. In short, whoever had seen us in our order, might sooner have expected the sky to fall, than that it should never have come to our turn. With this our sport was at an end, and we had to satisfy ourselves with the Virgin's waggery.

In the interim, the little wanton Cupid came in to us too. But we could not sport ourselves with him enough, because he presented himself on behalf of their Royal Majesties, and delivered us a health (from them) out of a golden cup, and had to call our virgins to the King, declaring also that he could at this time tarry no longer with them. So, with a due return of our most humble thanks we let him fly off again.

Now because (in the interim) the mirth had begun to fall to my consort's feet — and the virgins were not sorry to see it — they quickly started up a civil dance, which I beheld with pleasure rather than taking part; for my mercurialists were so ready with their postures, as if they had long been of the trade. After a few dances our president came in again, and told us how the artists and students had offered themselves to their Royal Majesties, for their honor and pleasure, to act a merry comedy before their departure; and if we thought it good to be present at this, and to wait upon their Royal Majesties to the House of the Sun, it would be acceptable to them, and they would most graciously acknowledge it. Hereupon in the first place we returned our most humble thanks for the honor vouchsafed us; not only this, but moreover we most submissively tendered our humble service.

This the Virgin related again, and presently brought word to attend their Royal Majesties (in our order) in the gallery, where we were soon led; and we did not stay long there, for the Royal Procession was just ready, yet without any music at all. The unknown Duchess who was with us yesterday went in front, wearing a small and costly coronet, appareled in white satin. She carried nothing but a small crucifix which was made of a pearl, and this very day wrought between the young King and his Bride. After her went the six aforementioned virgins in two ranks, who carried the King's jewels belonging to the little altar. Next to these came the three Kings. The Bridegroom was in the midst of them in a plain dress, but in black satin, after the Italian fashion. He had on a small round black hat, with a little pointed black feather, which he courteously took off to us, so to signify his favor towards us. We bowed ourselves to him, as also to the first, as we had been instructed before. After the Kings came the three Queens, two of whom were richly dressed, but she in the middle was likewise all in black, and Cupid held up her train. After this, intimation was given to us to follow, and after us the Virgins, till at last old Atlas brought up the rear.

In such procession, through many stately walks, we at length came to the House of the Sun, there next to the King and Queen, upon a richly furnished scaffold, to behold the previously ordained comedy. We indeed, though separated, stood on the right hand of the Kings, but the virgins stood on the left, except those to whom the Royal Ensigns were committed. To them was allotted their own place at the top of all. But the rest of the attendants had to stand below between the columns, and to be content with that.

Now because there are many remarkable passages in this comedy, I will not omit to go over it briefly.

First of all, a very ancient King came on, with some servants; before his throne was brought a little chest, with mention being made that it was found upon the water. Now it being opened, there appeared in it a lovely baby, together with some jewels, and a small letter of parchment sealed and superscribed to the King, which the King therefore opened; and having read it, wept, and then declared to his servants how injuriously the King of the Moors had deprived his aunt of her country, and had extinguished all the royal seed even to his infant, with the daughter of which country he had now the intention of matching his son. Hereupon he swore to maintain perpetual enmity with the Moor and his allies, and to revenge this upon them; and with this he commanded that the child should be tenderly nursed, and to make preparation against the Moor. Now this provision, and the disciplining of the young lady (who after she had grown up a little was committed to an ancient tutor) took up all the first act, with many very fine and laudable sports besides.

In the interlude a lion and griffin were set at one another to fight, and the lion got the victory, which was also a pretty sight.

In the second act, the Moor, a very black treacherous fellow, came on too. He, having with vexation understood that his murder had been discovered, and that a little lady was craftily stolen from him too, began thereupon to consult how by stratagem he might be able to encounter so powerful an adversary; on which he was eventually advised by certain fugitives who fled to him because of a famine.

So, the young lady, contrary to everyone's expectations, fell again into his hands; he would have been likely to have caused her to be slain if he had not been wonderfully deceived by his own servants. Thus, this act was concluded too, with a marvelous triumph of the Moor.

In the third act a great army of the King's party was raised against the Moor, and put under the conduct of an ancient valiant knight, who fell into the Moor's country, till at length he forcibly rescued the young lady from the tower, and appareled her anew. After this in a trice they erected a glorious scaffold, and placed their young lady upon it. Presently twelve royal ambassadors came, amongst whom the aforementioned knight made a speech, alleging that the King his most gracious lord had not only delivered her from death earlier, and even caused her to be royally brought up until now (though she had not behaved herself altogether as became her). But moreover, his Royal Majesty had, before others, elected her to be a spouse for the young lord his son, and most graciously desired that the said espousals might actually be executed, if they would be sworn to his Majesty upon the following articles. Hereupon out of a patent he caused certain glorious conditions to be read, which if it were not too long, would be well worthy of being recounted here. In brief, the young lady took an oath inviolably to observe the same, returning thanks too in a most seemly way for such a high grace. Whereupon they began to sing to the praise of God, of the King, and the young lady, and so for the time being departed.

For sport, in the meantime, the four beasts of Daniel, as he saw them in the vision and as he described them at length, were brought in, all of which had its certain signification.

In the fourth act the young lady was again restored to her lost kingdom, and crowned, and for a while, in this array, conducted about the place with extraordinary joy. After these many and various ambassadors presented themselves, not only to wish her prosperity, but also to behold her glory. Yet it was not for long that she preserved her integrity, but soon began again to look wantonly about her, and to wink at the ambassadors and lords; in this she truly acted her part.

These manners of hers were soon known to the Moor, who would by no means neglect such an opportunity, and because her steward did not pay sufficient attention to her, she was easily blinded with great promises, so that she did not keep good confidence with her King, but privately submitted herself entirely to the disposal of the Moor. Hereupon the Moor made haste, and having (by her consent) got her into his hands, he gave her good words until all her kingdom had subjected itself to him. After which, in the third scene of this act, he caused her to be led forth, and first to be stripped stark naked, and then to be bound to a post upon a scurvy wooden scaffold, and well scourged, and at last sentenced to death. This was so woeful a spectacle, that it made the eyes of many run over. Hereupon like this, naked as she was, she was cast into prison, there to await her death, which was to be procured by poison, which did not kill her, but made her leprous all over. Thus, this act was for the most part lamentable.

Between acts, they brought forth Nebuchadnezzar's image, which was adorned with all manner of arms, on the head, breast, belly, legs and feet, and the like, of which more shall be said in the future explanation.

In the fifth act the young King was told of all that had passed between the Moor and his future spouse; he first interceded with his father for her, entreating that she might not be left in that condition; which his father having agreed to, ambassadors were dispatched to comfort her in her sickness and captivity, but yet also to make her see her inconsiderateness. But she still would not receive them, but consented to be the Moor's concubine, which was also done, and the young King was acquainted with it.

After this came a band of fools, each of which brought with him a cudgel; within a trice they made a great globe of the world, and soon undid it again. It was a fine sportive fantasy.

In the sixth act the young King resolved to do battle with the Moor, which was also done. And although the Moor was discomforted, yet all held the young King too to be dead. At length he came to himself again, released his spouse, and committed her to his steward and chaplain. The first of these tormented her greatly; then the tables were turned, and the priest was so insolently wicked that he had to be above all, until this was reported to the young King; who hastily dispatched one who broke the neck of the priest's mightiness, and adorned the bride in some measure for the nuptials.

After the act a vast artificial elephant was brought forth. He carried a great tower with musicians, which was also well pleasing to all.

In the last act the bridegroom appeared with such pomp as cannot be believed, and I was amazed how it was brought to pass. The bride met him in similar solemnity, whereupon all the people cried out LONG LIVE THE BRIDEGROOM! LONG LIVE THE BRIDE! — so that by this comedy they also congratulated our King and Queen in the most stately manner, which (as I well observed) pleased them most extraordinarily well.

At length they walked about the stage in this procession, till at last they began to sing altogether as follows:

I
This lovely time
Brings much joy
With the king's wedding,
So, sing you all
That it resounds
And gladness be to him
Who gives it to us.

II
The beauteous bride
Whom we have long awaited
Shall be betrothed to him,
And we have won
Where after we did strive
O happy he
Who looks to himself.

III

The elders good
Are bidden now,
For Long they were in care,
In honor multiply
That thousands arise
From your own blood

After these thanks were returned, and the comedy was finished with joy, and the particular enjoyment of the Royal Persons, so (the evening also drawing near already) they departed together in their aforementioned order.

But we were to attend the Royal Persons up the winding stairs into the hall, where the tables were already richly furnished, and this was the first time that we were invited to the King's table. The little altar was placed in the midst of the hall, and the six royal ensigns previously mentioned were laid upon it. At this time the young King behaved himself very graciously towards us, yet he could not be heartily merry; although he now and then discoursed a little with us, yet he often sighed, at which the little Cupid only mocked, and played his waggish tricks. The old King and Queen were very serious; only the wife of one of the ancient Kings was gay enough, the reason for which I did not yet understand.

During this time, the Royal Persons took up the first table, at the second only we sat. At the third, some of the principal virgins placed themselves. The rest of the virgins, and men, all had to wait. This was performed with such state and solemn stillness that I am afraid to say very much about it.

But I cannot leave untouched upon here, how all the Royal Persons, before the meal, attired themselves in snow-white glittering garments, and so sat down at the table. Over the table hung the great golden crown, the precious stones of which would have sufficiently illuminated the hall without any other light. However, all the lights were kindled at the small taper upon the altar; what the reason was I did not know for sure. But I took very good notice of this, that the young King frequently sent meat to the white serpent upon the little altar, which caused me to muse.

Almost all the prattle at this banquet was made by little Cupid, who could not leave us (and me, indeed, especially) untormented. He was perpetually producing some strange matter. However, there was no considerable mirth, all went silently on; from which I, myself, could imagine some great imminent peril. For there was no music at all heard; but if we were demanded anything, we had to give short round answers, and so let it rest. In short, all things had so strange a face, that the sweat began to trickle down all over my body; and I am apt to believe that the most stout-hearted man alive would then have lost his courage.

Supper being now almost ended; the young King commanded the book to be reached him from the little altar. This he opened, and caused it once again to be propounded to us by an old man, whether we resolved to abide by him in prosperity and adversity; which we having consented to with trembling, he further had us asked, whether we would give him our hands on it, which, when we could find no evasion, had to be so. Hereupon one after another arose, and with his own hand wrote himself down in this book.

When this also had been performed, the little crystal fountain, together with a very small crystal glass, was brought near, out of which all the Royal Persons drank one after another. Afterwards it was held out to us too, and so to all persons; and this was called the Draught of Silence. Hereupon all the Royal Persons presented us their hands, declaring that if we did not now stick to them, we should nevermore from now on see them; which truly made our eyes run over. But our president engaged herself and promised a great deal on our behalf, which gave them satisfaction.

Meantime a little bell was rung, at which all the Royal Persons became so incredibly bleak, that we were ready to despair utterly. They quickly took off their white garments again, and put on entirely black ones. The whole hall likewise was hung about with black velvet, the floor was covered with black velvet, with which also the ceiling above was overspread (all this being prepared beforehand). After that the tables were also removed, and all seated themselves round about upon the form, and we also put on black habits. In came our president again, who had before gone out, and she brought with her six black taffeta scarves, with which she bound the six Royal Persons' eyes. Now when they could no longer see, six covered coffins were immediately brought in by the servants, and set down in the hall; also, a low black seat was placed in the middle. Finally, there came in a very coal-black, tall man, who bore in his hand a sharp axe. Now after the old King had first been brought to the seat, his head was instantly whipped off, and wrapped in a black cloth; but the blood was received into a great golden goblet, and placed with him in this coffin that stood by; which, being covered, was set aside. Thus, it went with the rest also, so that I thought it would at length have come to me too, but it did not. For as soon as the six Royal Persons were beheaded, the black man went out again; another followed after him, and beheaded him too just before the door, and brought back his head together with the axe, which were laid in a little chest.

This indeed seemed to me a bloody Wedding, but because I could not tell what was yet to happen, for the time being I had to suspend my understanding until I had further resolved things. For the Virgin too, seeing that some of us were faint-hearted and wept, bid us be content.

"For", she said to us, "The life of these now stands in your hands, and if you follow me, this death shall make many alive."

With this she intimated that we should go to sleep, and trouble ourselves no further on their part, for they should be sure to have their due right. And so, she bade us all goodnight, saying that she must watch the dead bodies this night. We did this, and were each of us conducted by our pages into our lodgings. My page talked with me of sundry and various matters (which I still remember very well) and gave me cause enough to admire his understanding. But his intention was to lull me to sleep, which at last I well observed; so, I made as though I was fast asleep, but no sleep came into my eyes, and I could not put the beheaded out of my mind.

Now my lodging was directly over against the great lake, so that I could easily look upon it, the windows being near to the bed. About midnight, as soon as it had struck twelve, suddenly I saw a great fire on the lake, so out of fear I quickly opened the window to see what would become of it. Then from afar I saw seven ships making forward, which were all full of lights. Above each of them on the top hovered a flame that passed to and fro, and sometimes descended right down, so that I could easily judge that it must be the spirits of the beheaded.

Now these ships gently approached land, and each of them had no more than one mariner. As soon as they had come to shore, I saw our Virgin with a torch going towards the ship, after whom the six covered coffins were carried, together with the little chest, and each of them was secretly laid in a ship.

So, I awakened my page too, who greatly thanked me, for, having run up and down a lot all day, he might have slept through this altogether, though he knew quite well about it. Now as soon as the coffins were laid in the ships, all the lights were extinguished, and the six flames passed back together over the lake, so that there was no more than one light in each ship for a watch. There were also some hundreds of watchmen who had encamped themselves on the shore, and sent the Virgin back again into the castle; she carefully bolted everything up again, so that I could judge that there was nothing more to be done this night, but that we must await the day.

So, we again took ourselves to rest. And I only of all my company had a chamber towards the lake, and saw this, so that now I was also extremely weary, and so fell asleep in my manifold speculations.

The Fifth Day

The night was over, and the dear wished-for day broke, when hastily I got out of bed, more desirous to learn what might yet ensue, than that I had slept enough. Now after I had put on my clothes, and according to my custom had gone down the stairs, it was still too early, and I found nobody else in the hall; so I entreated my page to lead me about a little in the castle, and show me something rare. He was now (as always) willing, and led me down certain steps underground, to a great iron door, on which the following words in copper letters were fixed:

(Here lies buried Venus, that beauty which has undone many a great man in fortune, honor, blessing and prosperity.)

This I thus copied, and set down in my table-book. Now after this door was opened, the page led me by the hand through a very dark passage, till we came again to a very little door, that was only now put to; for (as my page informed me) it was first opened yesterday when the coffins were taken out, and had not since been shut. Now as soon as we stepped in, I saw the most precious thing that Nature ever created, for this vault had no light other than that from certain huge great carbuncles, and this (as I was informed) was the King's Treasury. But the main and most glorious thing that I saw here was a sepulcher (which stood in the middle) so rich that I wondered that it was not better guarded. To which the page answered me, that I had good reason to be thankful to my planet, by whose influence it was that I had now seen certain pieces which no other human eye (except the King's family) had ever had a view of.

This sepulcher was triangular, and had in the middle of it a vessel of polished copper; the rest was of pure gold and precious stones. In the vessel stood an angel, who held in his arms an unknown tree, which continually dropped fruit into the vessel; and as often as the fruit fell into the vessel, it turned into water, and ran out from there into three small golden vessels standing by. This little altar was supported by these three animals, an eagle, an ox and a lion, which stood on an exceedingly costly base.

I asked my page what this might signify.

"Here," he said, *"lies buried Lady Venus, that beauty which has undone many a great man, both in fortune, honor, blessing and prosperity."* After which he showed me a copper door on the pavement.

"Here," he said, *"if you please, we may go further down."*

"I still follow you." I replied.

So, I went down the steps, where it was exceedingly dark, but the page immediately opened a little chest, in which stood a small ever-burning taper, at which he kindled one of the torches which lay by. I was greatly terrified, and seriously asked how he dared do this?

He said by way of answer

"As long as the Royal Persons are still at rest, we have nothing to fear."

Then I saw a rich bed ready-made, hung about with curious curtains, one of which he drew aside, where I saw the Lady Venus stark naked (for he threw up the covers too) lying there in such beauty, and in such a surprising fashion, that I was almost beside myself; neither do I yet know whether it was a piece thus carved, or a human corpse that lay dead there. For she was altogether immovable, and yet I dared not touch her. So, she was again covered, and the curtain drawn before her, yet she was still (as it were) in my eye. But I soon saw behind the bed a tablet on which it was written as follows:

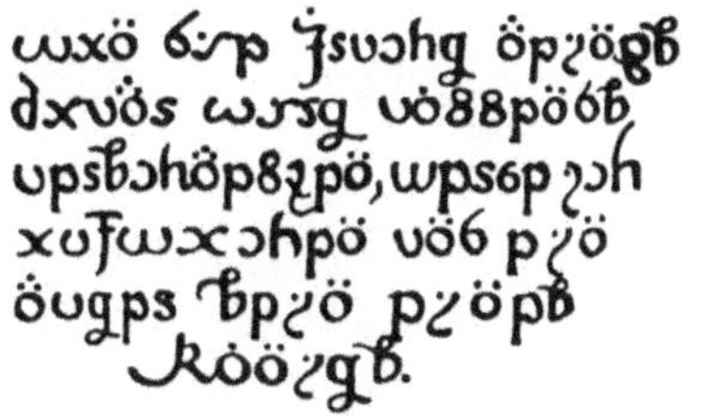

ᴡxö 6ʮp ᵗʃsʋɔhq öpᴢögß
dxʋös ᴡɹʃg ʋö�932pöö6ß
ʋpsß3höp8ᴢpö, ᴡpsᴇp ᴢʌh
xʋʃᴡxɔhpö ʋö6 pᴢö
öʋgps ᵗßpᴢö pᴢöpß
ᴊᴋööᴢgᵗß.

*(When the fruit of my tree shall be quite melted down
then I shall awake and be the Mother of a King.)*

I asked my page about this writing, but he laughed, with the promise that I should know it too. So, he putting out the torch, we ascended again. Then I had a better look at all the little doors, and first found that on every corner there burned a small taper of pyrites, of which I had before taken no notice, for the fire was so clear that it looked much more like a stone than a taper. From this heat the tree was forced continually to melt, yet it still produced new fruit. Now behold (said the page) what I heard revealed to the King by Atlas. When the tree (he said) shall be quite melted down, then shall Lady Venus awake, and be the mother of a King.

Whilst he was thus speaking, in flew the little Cupid, who at first was somewhat abashed at our presence, but seeing us both look more like the dead than the living, he could not in the end refrain from laughing, demanding what spirit had brought us there. I with trembling answered him, that I had lost my way in the castle, and had come here by chance, and that the page likewise had been looking up and down for me, and at last came upon me here, and I hoped he would not take it amiss.

"Well then, that's well enough yet, my old busy grandsire," said Cupid, *"but you might easily have served me a scurvy trick, had you been aware of this door. Now I must look better to it,"*

And so he put a strong lock on the copper door where we had before descended.

I thanked God that he had not come upon us sooner. My page too was happier, because I had helped him so well at this pinch.

"Yet," said Cupid, *"I cannot let it pass unrevenged that you were so near stumbling upon my dear mother."*

With that he put the point of his dart into one of the little tapers, and heating it a little, pricked me with it on the hand, which at that time I paid little attention to, but was glad that it had gone so well for us, and that we came off without further danger.

Meantime my companions had got out of bed too, and had returned into the hall again. To them I also joined myself, making as if I had just risen. After Cupid had carefully made all fast again, he came to us too, and would have me show him my hand, where he still found a little drop of blood; at which he heartily laughed, and bade the rest have a care of me, as I would shortly end my days. We all wondered how Cupid could be so merry, and have no sense at all of yesterday's sad occurrences. But he was in no way troubled.

Now our president had in the meantime made herself ready for the journey, coming in all in black velvet, yet she still carried her branch of laurel. Her virgins too had their branches. Now all things being ready, the Virgin asked us first to drink something, and then presently to prepare for the procession, so we did not tarry long but followed her out of the hall into the court. In the court stood six coffins, and my companions thought nothing other than that the six Royal Persons lay in them, but I well observed the device. Yet I did not know what was to be done with these others. By each coffin were eight muffled men. Now as soon as the music began (it was so mournful and dole-some a tune, that I was astonished at it) they took up the coffins, and we (as we were ordered) had to go after them into the aforementioned garden, in the middle of which was erected a wooden edifice, having round about the roof a glorious crown, and standing upon seven columns. Within it were formed six sepulchers, and by each of them was a stone; but in the middle was a round hollow rising stone. In these graves the coffins were quietly and with many ceremonies laid. The stones were shoveled over them, and they shut fast. But the little chest was to lie in the middle. Herewith my companions were deceived, for they imagined nothing other but that the dead corpses were there. Upon the top of all there was a great flag, having a phoenix painted on it, perhaps the more to delude us. Here I had great occasion to thank God that I had seen more than the rest.

Now after the funerals were done, the Virgin, having placed herself upon the middlemost stone, made a short oration, that we should be constant to our engagements, and not repine at the pains we were hereafter to undergo, but be helpful in restoring the present buried Royal Persons to life again; and therefore without delay to rise up with her, to journey to the tower of Olympus, to fetch from there medicines useful and necessary for this purpose.

This we soon agreed to, and followed her through another little door right

82

to the shore. There the seven aforementioned ships stood all empty, on which the virgins stuck up their laurel branches, and after they had distributed us in the six ships, they caused us thus to begin our voyage in God's name, and looked upon us as long as they could have us in sight, after which they, with all the watchmen, returned into the castle. Our ships each had a peculiar device. Five of them indeed had the five regular bodies, each their own, but mine, in which the Virgin sat too, carried a globe. Thus, we sailed on in a particular order, and each ship the Moor lay. In this were twelve musicians, who played excellently well, and its device was a pyramid. Next followed three abreast, B, C, and D, in which we were. I sat in C.

In the middle behind these came the two fairest and stateliest ships, E and F, stuck about with many branches of laurel, having no passengers in them; their flags were the sun and moon. But in the rear was only one ship, G; in this were forty virgins.

Now having passed over this lake in this way, we first went through a narrow arm, into the right seas, where all the sirens, nymphs, and sea-goddesses were waiting for us; wherefore they immediately dispatched a sea-nymph to us to deliver their present and offering of honor to the Wedding.

It was a costly, great, set, round and oriental pearl, the like of which has never been seen, neither in our world nor yet in the new world. Now the Virgin having friendlily received it, the nymph further entreated that audience might be given to their entertainments, and to make a little stand, which the Virgin was content to do, and commanded the two great ships to stand in the middle, and the rest to encompass them in a pentagon.

After which the nymphs fell into a ring about, and with a most delicate sweet voice began to sing as follows:

I

Naught better is on earth
Then lovely noble love
Whereby we be as God
And no one vexed his neighbor.
So, let unto the king be sung
That all the sea shall sound.
We ask, and answer you.

II

What had to us life brought?
'Tis Love
Who had brought grace again?
'Tis Love
Whence are we born?
Of Love
How were we all forlorn?
Without Love

III

Who had us then begotten?
'Twas Love
Wherefore were we suckled?
For Love
What owe we to our elders?
'Tis Love
And why are they so patient?
From Love

IV

What does all things o'ercome?
'Tis Love
Can we find Love as well?
Through Love
Where allows a man's good work appear?
In Love
Who can unite a twain?
'Tis Love

V

So, let us all sing
That it resounds
To honor Love
Which will increase
With our lord king and queen,
Their bodies are here, their souls are fled.

VI

And as we live
So shall God give
Where love and grace
Did sunder them
That we with flame of Love
May haply join them up again.

VII

So, shall this song
In greatest joy
Though thousand generations come
Return into eternity.

When they, with most admirable concert and melody, had finished this song, I no more wondered at Ulysses for stopping the ears of his companions, for I seemed to myself the most unhappy man alive, because nature had not made me, too, so trim a creature. But the Virgin soon dispatched them, and commanded us to set sail from there; so, the nymphs went off too, after they had been presented with a long red scarf for a gratuity, and dispersed themselves in the sea.

I was at this time aware that Cupid began to work with me too, which yet tended by a very little towards my credit, and forasmuch as my giddiness is not likely to be beneficial to the reader, I am resolved to let it rest as it is. But this was the very wound that in the first book I received on the head in a dream. And let everyone take warning by me of loitering about Venus' bed, for Cupid can by no means brook it.

After some hours, having gone a good way in friendly discourses, we came within sight of the Tower of Olympus, so the Virgin commanded to give the signal of our approach by the discharge of some pieces, which was also done. And immediately we saw a great white flag thrust out, and a small gilded pinnace sent forth to meet us. Now as soon as this had come to us, we perceived in it a very ancient man, the Warder of the Tower, with certain guards clothed in white, by whom we were friendlily received, and so conducted to the Tower.

This Tower was situated upon an island which was exactly square, and which was environed with a wall that was so firm and thick that I myself counted three hundred and sixty passes over. On the other side of the wall was a fine meadow with certain little gardens, in which grew strange, and to me unknown, fruits; and then again there was an inner wall about the Tower. The Tower itself was just as if seven round towers had been built one by another, yet the middlemost was somewhat the higher, and within they all entered one into another, and had seven stories one above another. Being come in this way to the gates of the Tower, we were led a little aside by the wall, so that, as I well observed, the coffins might be brought into the Tower without our taking notice; of this the rest knew nothing.

This being done, we were conducted into the Tower at the very bottom, which although it was excellently painted, yet we had little recreation there; for this was nothing but a laboratory, where we had to beat and wash plants, and precious stones, and all sorts of things, and extract their juice and essence, and put the same in glasses, and hand them over to be put aside. And truly our Virgin was so busy with us, and so full of her directions, that she knew how to give each of us enough employment, so that in this island we had to be mere drudges, till we had achieved all that was necessary for the restoring of the beheaded bodies.

Meantime (as I afterwards understood) three virgins were in the first apartment washing the bodies with all diligence. Now when we had at last almost finished this preparation of ours, nothing more was brought us but some broth with a little draught of wine, by which I well observed that we were not here for our pleasure. For when we had finished our day's work, too, everyone had only a mattress laid on the ground for him, with which we were to content ourselves.

For my part I was not very much bothered about sleeping, and therefore walked out into the garden, and at length came as far as the wall; and because the heaven was at that time very clear, I could well drive away the time in contemplating the stars. By chance I came to a great pair of stone stairs, which led up to the top of the wall. And because the moon shone very bright, I was so much the more confident, and went up, and looked a little upon the sea too, which was now exceedingly calm.

And thus, having good opportunity to consider more about astronomy, I found that this present night there would occur a conjunction of the planets, the like of which was not otherwise usually to be observed. Now having looked a good while at the sea, and it being just about midnight, as soon as it had struck twelve I saw from afar the seven flames passing over the sea towards here, and taking themselves towards the top of the spire of the Tower. This made me somewhat afraid, for as soon as the flames had settled themselves, the winds arose, and began to make the sea very tempestuous. The moon also was covered with clouds, and my joy ended with such fear that I scarcely had enough time to find the stairs ended with such fear that I scarcely had enough time to find the stairs again, and take myself to the Tower again. Now whether the flames tarried any longer, or passed away again, I cannot say, for in this obscurity I did not dare venture abroad more.

So, I lay down on my mattress, and there being in the laboratory a pleasant and gently murmuring fountain, I fell asleep so much the sooner. And thus, the fifth day too was concluded with wonders.

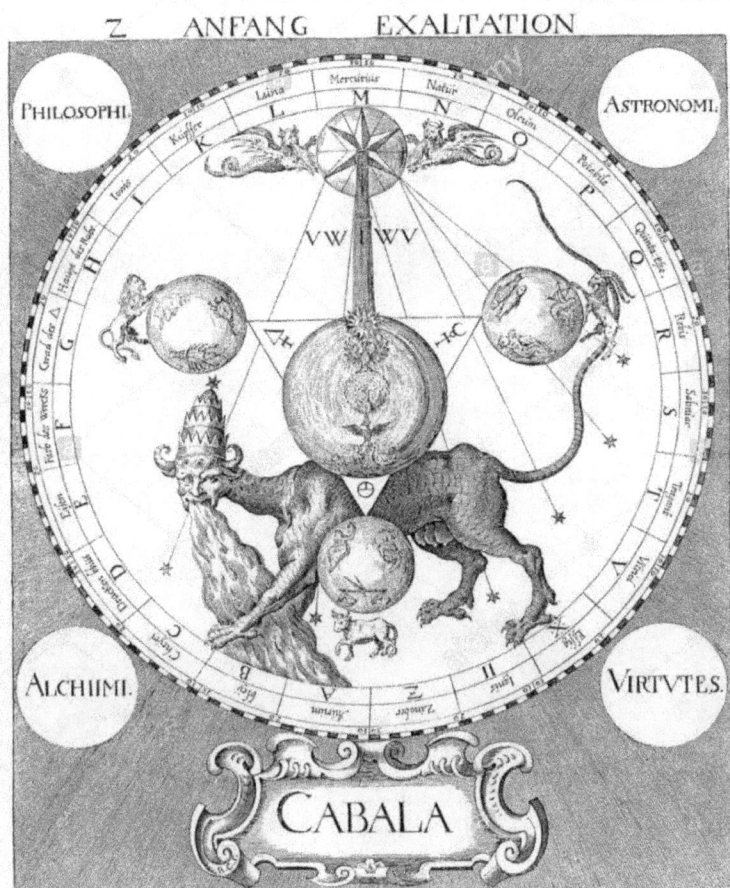

The Sixth Day

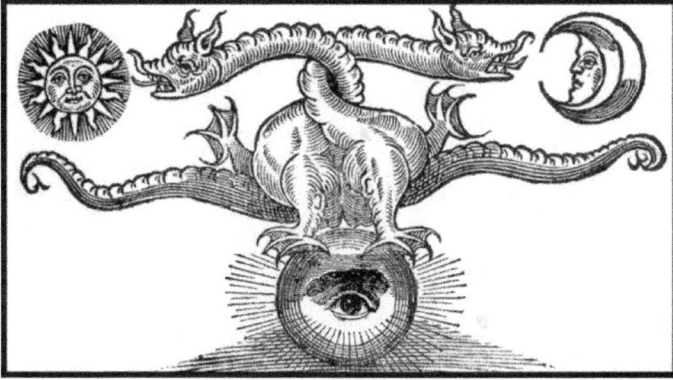

Next morning, after we had awakened one another, we sat together a while to discuss what might yet be the events to occur. For some were of the opinion that they should all be brought back to life again together. Others contradicted this, because the decease of the ancients was not only to restore life, but to increase it also to the young ones. Some imagined that they had not been put to death, but that others had been beheaded in their stead.

We now having talked together a pretty long while, in came the old man, and first saluting us, looked about him to see if all things were ready, and the processes sufficiently completed. We had so conducted ourselves as regards this that he had no fault to find with our diligence, so he placed all the glasses together, and put them into a case. Presently in came certain youths bringing with them some ladders, ropes, and large wings, which they laid down before us. Then the old man began as follows: "My dear sons, each of you must this day constantly bear one of these three things about with him. Now you are free either to make a choice of one of them, or to cast lots about it."

We replied, "we would choose".

"No," he said, "let it rather go by lot."

Hereupon he made three little schedules. On one he wrote 'Ladder', on the second 'Rope', on the third 'Wings'. These he put in a hat, and each man must draw, and whatever he got, that was to be his. Those who got the ropes imagined themselves to have the best of it, but I chanced to get a ladder, which afflicted me greatly, for it was twelve feet long, and pretty weighty, and I was forced to carry it, whereas the others could handsomely coil their ropes about them. And as for the wings, the old man joined them so closely onto the third group, as if they had grown upon them.

Hereupon he turned the cock, and then the fountain no longer ran, and we had to remove it from the middle out of the way. After all things were carried o?, he took leave, taking with him the casket with the glasses, and locked the door fast after him, so that we imagined nothing other but that we had been imprisoned in this Tower.

But it was hardly a quarter of an hour before a round hole at the very top was uncovered, where we saw our Virgin, who called to us, and bade us good morrow, desiring us to come up. Those with the wings were instantly above and through the hole. Only those with the ropes were in an evil plight. For as soon as every one of us was up, he was commanded to draw up the ladder after him. At last each man's rope was hanged on an iron hook, so everyone had to climb up by his rope as well as he could, which indeed was not accomplished without blisters.

Now as soon as we were all up, the hole was covered again, and we were friendlily received by the Virgin. This room was the whole breadth of the Tower itself, having six very stately vestries raised a little above the room, and were entered by an ascent of three steps. In these vestries we were placed, there to pray for the life of the King and Queen. Meanwhile the Virgin went in and out of the little door A, till we were ready.

For as soon as our process was absolved, there was brought in by twelve persons (who were formerly our musicians), through the little door, and placed in the middle, a wonderful thing of longish shape, which my companions took only to be a fountain. But I well observed that the corpses lay in it, for the inner chest was of an oval figure, so large that six persons might well lie in it one by another. After which they again went forth, fetched their instruments, and conducted in our Virgin, together with her female attendants, with a most delicate sound of music. The Virgin carried a little casket, but the rest only branches and small lamps, and some lighted torches too. The torches were immediately given into our hands, and we were to stand about the fountain in this order.

First stood the Virgin A with her attendants in a ring round-about with the lamps and branches C. Next stood we with our torches B, then the musicians A in a long rank; last of all the rest of the virgins D in another long rank too. Now where the virgins came from, whether they lived in the castle, or whether they had been brought in by night, I do not know, for all their faces were covered with delicate white linen, so that I could not recognize any of them.

Hereupon the Virgin opened the casket, in which there was a round thing wrapped up in a piece of green double taffeta. This she laid in the uppermost vessel, and then covered it with the lid, which was full of holes, and which had besides a rim through which she poured in some of the water which we had prepared the day before. Then the fountain began immediately to run, and to flow into the little vessel through four small pipes. Beneath the underneath vessel there were many sharp points, on which the virgins stuck their lamps, so that the heat might reach the vessel, and make the water boil. Now the water beginning to simmer, it fell in upon the bodies by many little holes at A, and was so hot that it dissolved them all, and turned them into liquor. But what the above-mentioned round wrapped-up thing was, my companions did not know, but I understood that it was the Moor's head, from which the water drew so great a heat. At A, round about the great vessel, there were again many holes, in which they stuck their branches. Now whether this was done of necessity, or only for ceremony, I do not know. However, these branches were continually besprinkled by the fountain, and from them it afterwards dropped into the vessel something of a deeper yellow. This lasted for nearly two hours, the fountain still constantly running by itself; but the longer it ran, the fainter it was.

Meantime the musicians went their way, and we walked up and down in the room, and truly the room was made in such a way that we had opportunity enough to pass away our time. There were, for images, paintings, clockworks, organs, springing fountains, and the like, nothing forgotten.

Now it was near the time when the fountain ceased, and would run no longer, when the Virgin commanded a round golden globe to be brought. But at the bottom of the fountain there was a tap, by which she let out all the matter that was dissolved by those hot drops (of which certain parts were then very red) into the globe. The rest of the water which remained above in the kettle was poured out. And so, this fountain (which had now become much lighter) was again carried forth. Now whether it was opened elsewhere, or whether anything of the bodies that was further useful yet remained, I dare not say for certain. But this I know, that the water that was emptied into the globe was much heavier than six, or even more of us, were well able to bear, although going by its bulk it should have seemed not too heavy for one man. Now this globe having been got out of doors with much ado, we again sat alone, but I perceiving a trampling overhead, had an eye to my ladder.

Here one might take notice of the strange opinions my companions had concerning this fountain, for they, imagining that the bodies lay in the garden of the castle, did not know what to make of this kind of working, but I thanked God that I had awakened at so opportune a time, and that I had seen that which helped me the better in all the Virgin's business.

After one quarter of an hour the cover above was again lifted off, and we were commanded to come up, which was done as before with wings, ladders and ropes. And it vexed me not a little that whereas the virgins could go up another way, we had to take so much toil; yet I could well judge that there must be some special reason for it, and we must leave something for the old man to do too. For even those with wings had no advantage by them other than when they had to climb through the hole.

Now we having got up there, and the hole having been shut again, I saw the globe hanging by a strong chain in the middle of the room. In this room was nothing but windows, and between two windows there was a door, which was covered with nothing other than a great polished looking glass. And these windows and these looking-glasses were optically opposed to one another, so that although the sun (which was now shining exceedingly brightly) beat only upon one door, yet (after the windows towards the sun were opened, and the doors before the looking-glasses drawn aside) in all quarters of the room there were nothing but suns, which by artificial refractions beat upon the whole golden globe standing in the midst; and because (besides all this brightness) it was polished, it gave such a luster, that none of us could open our eyes, but were forced to look out of the windows till the globe was well heated, and brought to the desired effect. Here I may well avow that in these mirrors I have seen the most wonderful spectacle that ever Nature brought to light, for there were suns in all places, and the globe in the middle shined still brighter, so that we could no more endure it than the sun itself, except for one twinkling of an eye.

At length the Virgin commanded the looking glasses to be shut up again, and the windows to be made fast, and so to let the globe cool again a little; and this was done about seven o'clock. This we thought good, since we might now have a little leisure to refresh ourselves with breakfast. This treatment was again right philosophical, and we had no need to be afraid of intemperance, yet we had no want. And the hope of the future joy (with which the Virgin continually comforted us) made us so jocund that we took no notice of any pains or inconvenience. And this I can truly say too concerning my companions of high quality, that their minds never ran after their kitchen or table, but their pleasure was only to attend upon this adventurous physic, and hence to contemplate the Creator's wisdom and omnipotency.

After we had taken our meal, we again settled down to work, for the globe, which with toil and labor we were to lift off the chain and set upon the floor, was sufficiently cooled. Now the dispute was how to get the globe in half, for we were commanded to divide it in the middle. The conclusion was that a sharp pointed diamond would best do it. Now when we had thus opened the globe, there was nothing more of redness to be seen, but a lovely great snow-white egg. It made us rejoice most greatly that this had been brought to pass so well. For the Virgin was in perpetual care lest the shell might still be too tender. We stood round about this egg as jocund as if we ourselves had laid it. But the Virgin made it be carried forth, and departed herself, too, from us again, and (as always) locked the door. But what she did outside with the egg, or whether it was in some way privately handled, I do not know, neither do I believe it. Yet we were again to wait together for a quarter of an hour, till the third hole was opened, and we by means of our instruments came to the fourth stone or floor.

In this room we found a great copper vessel filled with yellow sand, which was warmed by a gentle fire. Afterwards the egg was raked up in it, that it might therein come to perfect maturity. This vessel was exactly square; upon one side stood these two verses, written in great letters.

O. BLI. TO. BIT. MI. LI.

On the second side were these three words:

SANITAS. NIX. HASTA.
(Health, Snow, Lance.)

The third had only one word:

F.I.A.T.

But on the behind was an entire inscription running thus:

QUOD.
Ignis: Aer: Aqua: Terra:
SANCTIS REGUM ET REGINARUM NOSTR:
Cineribus.
Eripere non potuerunt
Fidelis Chymicorum Turba
IN HANC URNAM
Contulit.

The Sixth Day

What
Fire: Air: Water: Earth
Were unable to rob
From the holy ashes
OF OUR KINGS AND QUEENS

Was gathered by the faithful flock
Of Alchemists
In this urn
A.D. 1459.

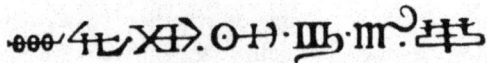

Now whether the egg was hereby meant, I leave to the learned to dispute; yet I do my part, and omit nothing undeclared. Our egg being now ready was taken out, but it needed no cracking, for the bird that was in it soon freed himself, and showed himself very jocund, yet he looked very bloody and without shape. We first set him upon the warm sand, so the Virgin commanded that before we gave him anything to eat, we should be sure to make him fast, otherwise he would give us all work enough. This being done too, food was brought him, which surely was nothing else than the blood of the beheaded, diluted again with prepared water; by which the bird grew so fast under our eyes, that we saw well why the Virgin gave us such warning about him. He bit and scratched so devilishly about him, that could he have had his will upon any of us, he would have dispatched him.

Now he was wholly black, and wild, so other food was brought him, perhaps the blood of another of the Royal Persons; whereupon all his black feathers molted again, and instead of them there grew out snow-white feathers. He was somewhat tamer too, and more docile. Nevertheless, we did not yet trust him. At the third feeding his feathers began to be so curiously colored that in all my life I never saw such beautiful colors. He was also exceedingly tame, and behaved himself so friendlily with us, that (the Virgin consenting) we released him from his captivity.

Our Virgin began:

"Since by your diligence, and our old man's consent, the bird has attained both his life and the highest perfection, this is a good reason that he should also be joyfully consecrated by us."

Herewith she commanded that dinner should be brought, and that we should again refresh ourselves, since the most troublesome part of our work was now over, and it was fitting that we should begin to enjoy our past labors. We began to make ourselves merry together. However, we still had all our mourning clothes on, which seemed somewhat reproachful to our mirth. Now the Virgin was perpetually inquisitive, perhaps to find to which of us her future purpose might prove serviceable. But her discourse was for the most part about Melting; and it pleased her well when one seemed expert in such compendious manuals as do particularly commend an artist. This dinner lasted not more than three quarters of an hour, which we still for the most part spent with our bird, and we had to constantly feed him with his food, but he remained much the same size. After dinner we were not allowed long to digest our food, before the Virgin, together with the bird, departed from us.

The fifth room was set open to us, where we went as before, and offered our services. In this room a bath was prepared for our bird, which was so colored with a fine white powder that it had the appearance of milk. Now it was at first cool when the bird was set into it. He was mighty well pleased with it, drinking of it, and pleasantly sporting in it. But after it began to heat because of the lamps that were placed under it, we had enough to do to keep him in the bath. We therefore clapped a cover on the vessel, and allowed him to thrust his head out through a hole, till he had in this way lost all his feathers in the bath, and was as smooth as a new-born child; yet the heat did him no further harm, at which I much marveled, for the feathers were completely consumed in this bath, and the bath was thereby tinged blue. At length we gave the bird air, and he sprang out of the vessel of his own accord, and he was so glitteringly smooth that it was a pleasure to behold. But because he was still somewhat wild, we had to put a collar with a chain about his neck, and so led him up and down the room. Meanwhile a strong fire was made under the vessel, and the bath boiled away till it all came down to a blue stone, which we took out, and having first pounded it, ground it with a stone, and finally with this color began to paint the bird's skin all over. Now he looked much stranger, for he was all blue, except the head, which remained white.

Herewith our work on this storey was performed, and we (after the Virgin with her blue bird was departed from us) were called up through the hole to the sixth storey, where we were greatly troubled. For in the middle was placed a little altar, in every way like that in the King's hall above described. Upon this stood the six aforementioned particulars, and he himself (the bird) made the seventh. First of all, the little fountain was set before him, out of which he drunk a good draught. Afterwards he pecked the white serpent until she bled a great deal. This blood we had to receive into a golden cup, and pour it down the bird's throat, who was greatly averse to it. Then we dipped the serpent's head in the fountain, upon which she revived again, and crept into her death's-head, so that I saw her no more for a long time after. Meantime, the sphere turned constantly, until it made the desired conjunction. Immediately the watch struck one, upon which another conjunction was set going. Then the watch struck two.

Finally, while we were observing the third conjunction, and this was indicated by the watch, the poor bird submissively laid down his neck upon the book of his own accord, and willingly allowed his head to be smitten off (by one of us chosen for this by lot). However, he yielded not a drop of blood until his breast was opened, and then the blood spurted out so fresh and clear as if it had been a fountain of rubies. His death went to our hearts, and yet we could well judge that a naked bird would stand us in little stead. So we let it be, and moved the little altar away and assisted the Virgin to burn the body to ashes (together with the little tablet hanging by) with fire kindled by the little taper; and afterwards to cleanse the same several times, and to lay them in a box of cypress wood.

Here I cannot conceal what a trick was played on myself and three others. After we had thus diligently taken up the ashes, the Virgin began to speak as follows:

"My lords, here we are in the sixth room, and we have only one more before us, in which our trouble will be at an end, and then we shall return home again to our castle, to awaken our most gracious Lords and Ladies. Now I could heartily wish that all of you, as you are here together, had behaved yourselves in such a way that I might have commended to our most renowned King and Queen, and you might have obtained a suitable reward; yet contrary to my desire, I have found amongst you these four lazy and sluggish workers (herewith she pointed at me and three others). Yet, according to my goodwill to each and every one, I am not willing to deliver them up to deserved punishment. However, so that such negligence may not remain wholly unpunished, I am resolved thus concerning them, that they shall only be excluded from the future seventh and most glorious action of all the rest, and so they shall incur no further blame from their Royal Majesties."

In what a state we now were at this speech I leave others to consider. For the Virgin knew so well how to keep her countenance, that the water soon ran over our baskets, and we esteemed ourselves the most unhappy of all men. After this the Virgin caused one of her maids (of whom there were many always at hand) to fetch the musicians, who were to blow us out of doors with cornets, with such scorn and derision that they themselves could hardly blow for laughing. But it afflicted us particularly greatly that the Virgin so vehemently laughed at our weeping, anger and impatience, and that there might well be some amongst our companions who were glad of this misfortune of ours.

But it proved otherwise, for as soon as we had come out of the door, the musicians told us to be of good cheer and follow them up the winding stairs. They led us up to the seventh floor under the roof, where we found the old man, whom we had not hitherto seen, standing upon a little round furnace. He received us friendlily, and heartily congratulated us that we had been chosen for this by the Virgin; but after he understood the fright we had received, his belly was ready to burst with laughing that we had taken such good fortune so badly.

"Hence," said he, "*my dear sons, learn that man never knows how well God intended him.*"

During this discourse the Virgin also came running in with her little box, and (after she had laughed at us enough) emptied her ashes into another vessel, and filled hers again with other stuff, saying she must now go and cast a mist before the other artists' eyes, and that we in the meantime should obey the old lord in whatsoever he commanded us, and not remit our former diligence. Herewith she departed from us into the seventh room into which she called our companions. Now what she did first with them there, I cannot tell, for not only were they most earnestly forbidden to speak of it, but we also, because of our work, did not dare peep on them through the ceiling.

But this was our work. We had to moisten the ashes with our previously prepared water until they became altogether like a very thin dough, after which we set the matter over the fire, till it was well heated. Then we cast it, hot like this, into two little forms or moulds, and let it cool a little.

Here we had leisure to look a while at our companions through certain crevices made in the floor. They were now very busy at a furnace, and each had to blow up the fire himself with a pipe, and they stood blowing about it like this, as if they were wondrously preferred before us in this. And this blowing lasted until our old man roused us to our work again, so that I cannot say what was done afterwards.

We opened our little forms, and there appeared two beautiful, bright and almost transparent little images, the like of which man's eye never saw, a male and a female, each of them only four inches long, and what surprised us most greatly was that they were not hard, but lithe and fleshy, like other human bodies, yet they had no life; so that I most assuredly believe that the Lady Venus's image was also made after some such manner.

These angelically fair babes we first laid upon two little satin cushions, and looked at them for a good while, till we were almost besotted by such exquisite objects. The old lord warned us to forbear, and continually to instill the blood of the bird (which had been received into a little golden cup) drop after drop into the mouths of the little images, from which they appeared to increase; and whereas they were before very small, they were now (according to proportion) much more beautiful, so that all painters ought to have been here, and would have been ashamed of their art in respect of these productions of nature. Now they began to grow so big that we lifted them from the little cushions, and had to lay them upon a long table, which was covered with white velvet. The old man also commanded us to cover them over up to the breast with a piece of the fine white double taffeta, which, because of their unspeakable beauty, almost went against us. But to be brief, before we had quite used up the blood in this way, they were already in their perfect full growth. They had golden-yellow, curly hair, and the above-mentioned figure of Venus was nothing to them.

But there was not yet any natural warmth or sensibility in them. They were dead figures, yet of a lively and natural color; and since care was to be taken that they did not grow too big, the old man would not permit anything more to be given to them, but covered their faces too with the silk, and caused the table to be stuck round-about with torches. Here I must warn the reader not to imagine these lights to have been put there out of necessity, for the old man's intent hereby was only that we should not observe when the soul entered into them; and indeed we should not have noticed it, had I not twice before seen the flames. However, I permitted the other three to remain with their own belief, neither did the old man know that I had seen anything more. Hereupon he asked us to sit down on a bench over against the table.

Presently the Virgin came in too, with the music and all necessities, and carried two curious white garments, the like of which I had never seen in the castle, nor can I describe them, for I thought that they were nothing other than crystal; but they were soft, and not transparent; so that I cannot describe them. These she laid down on a table, and after she had disposed her virgins upon a bench round about, she and the old man began many slight-of-hand tricks about the table, which was done only to blind us. This (as I told you) was managed under the roof, which was wonderfully formed; for on the inside it was arched into seven hemispheres, of which the middlemost was somewhat the highest, and had at the top a little round hole, which was nevertheless shut, and was observed by no one else.

After many ceremonies six virgins came in, each of whom carried a large

98

trumpet, around which were rolled a green, glittering and burning material like a wreath. The old man took one of these, and after he had removed some of the lights at the top of the table, and uncovered their faces, he placed one of the trumpets upon the mouth of one of the bodies in such a way that the upper and wider end of it was directed just towards the afore-mentioned hole. Here my companions always looked at the images, but I had other thoughts, for as soon as the foliage or wreath about the shank of the trumpet was kindled, I saw the hole at the top open, and a bright stream of fire shooting down the tube, and passing into the body; whereupon the hole was covered again, and the trumpet removed. With this device my companions were deluded, so that they imagined that life came into the image by means of the fire of the foliage, for as soon as he received the soul his eyes twinkled, although he hardly stirred. The second time he placed another tube upon its mouth, and kindled it again, and the soul was let down through the tube. This as repeated for each of them three times, after which all the lights were extinguished and carried away. The velvet coverings of the table were cast over them, and immediately a birthing bed was unlocked and made ready, into which, thus wrapped up, they were born. And after the coverings were taken off them, they were neatly laid by each other, and with the curtains drawn before them, they slept a good while.

Now, it was also time for the Virgin to see how other artists behaved themselves. They were well pleased because, as the Virgin afterwards informed me, they were to work in gold, which is indeed a piece of this art, but not the most principal, most necessary, and best. They had indeed too a part of these ashes, so that they imagined nothing other than that the whole bird was provided for the sake of gold, and that life must thereby be restored to the deceased.

Meantime we sat very still, waiting for our married couple to awake. About half an hour was spent like this. Then the wanton Cupid presented himself again, and after he had saluted us all, flew to them behind the curtain, tormenting them until they awakened. This was a cause of great amazement to them, for they imagined that they had slept from the very hour in which they were beheaded until now. Cupid, after he had awakened them, and renewed their acquaintance with one another, stepped aside a little, and allowed the two of them to get themselves together a bit better, meantime playing his tricks with us; and at length he wanted to have the music brought in, to be somewhat merrier.

Not long after, the Virgin herself came in, and after she had most humbly saluted the young King and Queen (who found themselves rather faint) and kissed their hands, she brought them the two strange garments, which they put on, and so stepped forth. Now there were already prepared two very strange chairs, in which they placed themselves. And they were congratulated with most profound reverence by us, for which the King himself most graciously returned his thanks, and again reassured us of all grace.

It was already about five o'clock, so they could no longer stay, but as soon as the best of their furniture could be laden, we had to attend the young Royal Persons down the winding stairs, through all doors and watches to the ship. In this they embarked, together with certain virgins and Cupid, and sailed so very swiftly that we soon lost sight of them; but they were met (as I was informed) by certain stately ships. Thus, in four hours' time they had gone many leagues out to sea. After five o'clock the musicians were charged to carry all things back again to the ships, and to make themselves ready for the voyage. But because this took rather a long time, the old lord commanded a party of his concealed soldiers to come out. They had hitherto been planted in a wall, so that we had not noticed any of them, whereby I observed that this Tower was well provided against opposition. Now these soldiers made quick work with our stuff, so that nothing more remained to be done but to go to supper.

The table being completely furnished, the Virgin brought us again to our companions, where we were to carry ourselves as if we had truly been in a lamentable condition, and forbear laughing. But they were always smiling to one another, although some of them sympathized with us too. At this supper the old lord was also with us, who was a most sharp inspector over us; for no-one could propound anything so discreetly, but he knew either how to confute it, or to amend it, or at least to give some good information on it. I learned a great deal from this lord, and it would be very good if each one would apply themselves to him, and take notice of his procedure, for then things would not miscarry so often and so unfortunately.

After we had taken our nocturnal refreshment, the old lord took us into his closets of rarities, which were dispersed here and there amongst the bulwarks; where we saw such wonderful productions of Nature, and other things too which man's wit, in imitation of Nature, had invented, that we needed another year to survey them sufficiently. Thus, we spent a good part of the night by candlelight. At last, because we were more inclined to sleep than to see many rarities, we were lodged in rooms in the wall, where we had not only costly and good beds, but also extraordinarily handsome chambers, which made us wonder all the more why we were forced to undergo so many hardships the day before. In this chamber I had good rest, and being for the most part without care, and weary with continual labor, the gentle rushing of the sea helped me to a sound and sweet sleep, for I continued in one dream from eleven o'clock till eight in the morning.

The Seventh Day

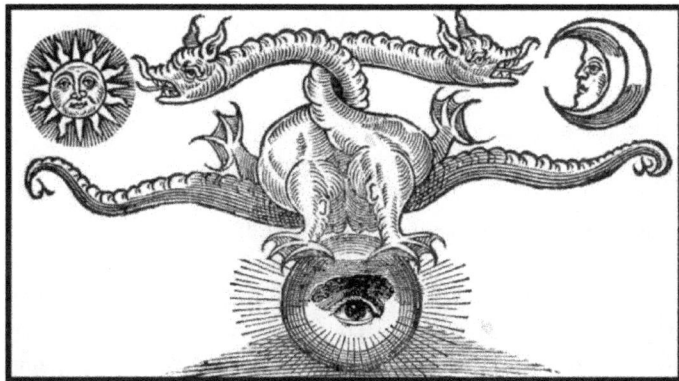

After eight o'clock I woke up, and quickly made myself ready, wanting to return again into the Tower; but the dark passages in the wall were so many and various, that I wandered a good while before I could find the way out. The same happened to the rest too, till at last we all met again in the nethermost vault, and entirely yellow apparel was given to us, together with our golden fleeces. At this time the Virgin declared to us that we were Knights of the Golden Stone, of which we were before ignorant.

After we had made ourselves ready, and taken our breakfast, the old man presented each of us with a medal of gold.

On one side were these words:

AR. NAT. MI.
(Art is the Priestess of Nature)

On the other these:

TEM. NA. F.
(Nature is the Daughter of Time.)

He exhorted us moreover that we should try to take nothing more than this token of remembrance. Herewith we went forth to the sea, where our ships lay, so richly equipped that it was not possible but that such amazing things must first have been brought there. The ships were twelve in number, six of ours, and six of the old lord's, who caused his ships to be freighted with well-appointed soldiers. But he himself came to us in our ship, where we were all together. In the first the musicians, of which the old lord also had a great number, seated themselves; they sailed before us to shorten the time. Our flags were the twelve celestial signs, and we sat in Libra. Besides other things our ship also had a noble and curious clock, which showed us all the minutes. The sea was so calm, too, that it was a singular pleasure to sail. But what surpassed all the rest was the old man's discourse; he knew so well how to pass away our time with wonderful stories, that I could have been content to sail with him all my life long.

Meanwhile the ships passed on in haste, for before we had sailed two hours the mariner told us that he already saw the whole lake almost covered with ships, by which we could conjecture that they had come out to meet us, which proved true. For as soon as we had come out of the sea into the lake by the aforementioned river, there before us were five hundred ships, one of which sparkled with gold and precious stones, and in which sat the King and Queen, together with other lords, ladies, and virgins of high birth. As soon as they were well in sight of us the pieces were discharged on both sides, and there was such a din of trumpets, shalms, and kettle drums that all the ships upon the sea capered again. Finally, as soon as we came near they brought our ships together, and so made a stand.

Immediately the old Atlas stepped forth on the King's behalf, making a short but handsome oration, in which he welcomed us, and asked whether the Royal Presents were ready. The rest of my companions were in great amazement, where this King should come from, for they imagined nothing other than that they would have to awaken him again. We allowed them to continue in their amazement, and acted as if it seemed strange to us too. After Atlas' oration out stepped our old man, making a rather longer reply, in which he wished the King and Queen all happiness and increase, after which he delivered up a curious small casket. What was in it, I do not know, but it was committed to Cupid to keep, who hovered between the King and Queen.

After the oration was finished, they again let off a joyful volley of shot, and so we sailed on a good time together, till at length we arrived at another shore. This was near the first gate at which I first entered. At this place again there attended a great multitude of the King's family together with some hundreds of horses. Now as soon as we came to shore, and disembarked, the King and Queen presented their hands to all of us, everyone, with singular kindness; and so, we were to get up on horseback.

Here I wish to friendlily entreat the reader not to interpret the following narration as any vain glory or pride of mine, but to credit me this much, that if there had not been a special necessity for it, I could very well have utterly concealed this honor which was shown me. We were all one after another distributed amongst the lords. But our old lord, and I, most unworthy, were to ride alongside the King, each of us bearing a snow- white ensign with a red cross. Indeed, I was made use of because of my age, for we both had long grey beards and hair. I had also fastened my tokens about my hat, which the young King soon noticed, and asked if I were he who could redeem these tokens at the gate?

I answered in most humble manner, *"Yes"*.

But he laughed at me, saying,

"There was no need for ceremony; I was HIS father."

Then he asked me with what I had redeemed them. I replied,

"With Water and Salt."

Whereupon he wondered who had made me so wise; upon which I grew a bit more confident, and recounted to him how it had happened with my bread, the Dove and the Raven, and he was pleased with it and said expressly that it must be that God had herein vouchsafed me a singular happiness.

With this we came to the first gate where the Porter with the blue clothes waited, bearing in his hand a supplication. Now as soon as he saw me alongside the King, he delivered me the supplication, most humbly beseeching me to mention his ingenuity to the King. Now in the first place I asked the King what the condition of this porter was. He friendlily answered me, that he was a very famous and rare astrologer, and always in high regard with the Lord his Father, but having once committed a fault against Venus, and seen her in her bed of rest, this punishment was therefore imposed upon him, that he should wait at the first gate for so long until someone should release him from it.

I replied,

"May he then be released?"

"Yes," said the King, *"if anyone can be found that has transgressed as highly as himself, he must take his place, and the other shall be free."*

103

This went to my heart, for my conscience convinced me that I was the offender, yet I kept quiet, and herewith delivered the supplication. As soon as he had read it, he was greatly terrified, so that the Queen (who with our virgins, and that other Duchess as well — whom I mentioned at the hanging of the weights — rode just behind us) observed this, and therefore asked him what this letter might mean. But he had no mind to take any notice of it, and putting away the paper, began to talk about other matters, till thus in about three hours' time we came to the castle, where we alighted, and waited upon the King as he went into his hall.

Immediately the King called for the old Atlas to come to him in a little closet, and showed him the writing, and Atlas did not tarry, but rode out again to the Porter to get more information on the matter. After this the young King, with his spouse, and the other lords, ladies and virgins, sat down. Then our Virgin began to highly commend the diligence we had shown, and the pains and labor we had undergone, requesting that we might be royally rewarded, and that she might be permitted to enjoy the benefit of her commission from then on. Then the old lord stood up too, and attested that all the Virgin had said was true, and that it was only just that we should both be contented on both our parts. Hereupon we were to step forward a little, and it was concluded that each man should make some possible wish, and accordingly obtain it; for it was not to be doubted that those of understanding would also make the best wish. So, we were to consider it until after supper.

Meantime the King and Queen, for recreation's sake, began to play together, at something which looked not unlike chess, only it had different rules; for it was the Virtues and Vices one against another, and it might ingeniously be observed with what plots the Vices lay in wait for the Virtues, and how to re-encounter them again. This was so properly and cleverly performed, that it is to be wished that we had the same game too. During the game, in came Atlas again, and made his report in private, but I blushed all over, for my conscience gave me no rest.

After this the King gave me the supplication to read, and the contents of it were much to this purpose. First he (the doorkeeper) wished the King prosperity, and increase, and that his seed might be spread abroad far and wide. Afterwards he remonstrated that the time was now come in which according to the royal promise he ought to be released, because Venus had already been uncovered by one of his guests, for his observations could not lie to him. And that if his Majesty would be pleased to make a strict and diligent enquiry, he would find that she had been uncovered, and if this should not prove to be so, he would be content to remain before the gate all the days of his life. Then he asked in the most humble manner, that upon peril of body and life he might be permitted to be present at this night's supper. He was hoping to seek out the very offender, and obtain his desired freedom. This was expressly and handsomely indicated, by which I could well perceive his ingenuity, but it was too sharp for me, and I would not have minded if I had never seen it. Now I was wondering whether he might perhaps be helped through my wish, so I asked the King whether he might not be released some other way.

"No," replied the King, "*because there is a special consideration in the business. However, for this night, we may well gratify him in his desire.*"

So, he sent someone to fetch him in. Meanwhile the tables were prepared in a spacious room, in which we had never been before, which was so perfect, and contrived in such a manner, that it is not possible for me even to begin to describe it. We were conducted into this with singular pomp and ceremony. Cupid was not at this time present, for (as I was informed) the disgrace which had happened to his mother had somewhat angered him. In brief, my offence, and the supplication which was delivered, were an occasion of much sadness, for the King was in perplexity how to make inquisition amongst his guests, and the more so because through this, even they who were yet ignorant of the matter would come to know about it. So, he caused the Porter himself, who had already arrived, to make his strict survey, and he himself acted as pleasantly as he was able.

However, eventually they all began to be merry again, and to talk to one another with all sorts of creative and profitable discourses. Now, how the treatment and other ceremonies were then performed, it is not necessary to declare, since it is neither the reader's concern, nor serviceable to my design. But all exceeded more in art, and human invention, than we exceeded in drinking! And this was the last and noblest meal at which I was present. After the banquet the tables were suddenly taken away, and certain curious chairs placed round about in a circle, in which we, together with the King and Queen, and both their old men and the ladies and virgins, were to sit.

After this, a very handsome page opened the above-mentioned glorious little book, and Atlas immediately placed himself in the midst, and began to speak to this purpose: that his Royal Majesty had not forgotten the service we had done him, and how carefully we had attended to our duty, and therefore by way of retribution had elected all and each of us Knights of the Golden Stone. And that it was therefore further necessary not only once again to oblige ourselves towards his Royal Majesty, but also to vow to the following articles; and then his Royal Majesty would likewise know how to behave himself towards his liege people. Upon which he caused the page to read over the articles, which were these.

(1) You my lords the Knights shall swear that you shall at no time ascribe your order to any devil or spirit, but only to God your Creator, and his handmaid Nature.

(2) That you will abominate all whoredom, incontinency and uncleanness, and not defile your order with such vices.

(3) That you through your talents will be ready to assist all that are worthy, and have need of them.

(4) That you desire not to employ this honor to worldly pride and high authority.

(5) That you shall not be willing to live longer than God will have you do. At this last article we could not choose but laugh, and it may well have been placed after the rest only for a conceit. Now after vowing to them all by the King's scepter, we were afterwards installed Knights with the usual ceremonies, and amongst other privileges set over Ignorance, Poverty, and Sickness, to handle them at our pleasure. And this was afterwards ratified in a little chapel (to which we were conducted in procession) and thanks returned to God for it. I also hung up there at that time my golden fleece and hat, and left them there for an eternal memorial, to the honor of God. And because everyone had to write his name there, I wrote thus:

The highest wisdom is to know nothing.
Brother Christian Rosenkreutz
Knight of the Golden Stone
A.D. 1459.

Others wrote likewise, each as it seemed good to him. After this, we were again brought into the hall, where, having sat down, we were admonished quickly to think what we each one would wish. But the King and his party retired into a little closet, there to give audience to our wishes. Now each man was called in separately, so that I cannot speak of any man's own wish. I thought nothing could be more praiseworthy than to demonstrate some laudable virtue in honor of my order, and found too that none at present could be better, and cost me more trouble, than Gratitude. Where-fore in spite of the fact that I might well have wished something dearer and more agreeable to myself, I vanquished myself, and concluded, even at my own peril, to free the Porter, my benefactor.

So, as I was now called in, I was first of all asked whether, having read the supplication, I had observed or suspected nothing concerning the offender? Upon which I began undauntedly to relate how all the business had passed, how through ignorance I fell into that mistake, and so offered myself to undergo all that I had thereby deserved. The King, and the rest of the lords, wondered greatly at so unexpected a confession, and so asked me to step aside a little.

Now as soon as I was called in again, Atlas declared to me that although it was grievous to the King's Majesty that I, whom he loved above others, had fallen into such a mischance, yet because it was not possible for him to transgress his ancient usages, he did not know how to absolve me; the other must be at liberty, and I put in his place; yet he would hope that some other would be apprehended, so that I might be able to go home again. However, no release was to be hoped for, till the marriage feast of his future son.

This sentence had nearly cost me my life, and I first hated myself and my twaddling tongue, in that I could not keep quiet; yet at last I took courage, and because I thought there was no remedy, I related how this Porter had bestowed a token on me, and commended me to the other, by whose assistance I stood upon the scale, and so was made partaker of all the honor and joy already received. And therefore now it was but fair that I should show myself grateful to my benefactor, and because this could not be done in any other way, I returned thanks for the sentence, and was willing gladly to bear some inconvenience for the sake of he who had been helpful to me in coming to such a high place. But if by my wish anything might be affected, I wished myself at home again, so that he by me, and I by my wish might be at liberty. Answer was made me, that the wishing did not stretch so far. However, I might wish him free. Yet it was very pleasing to his Royal Majesty that I had behaved myself so generously in this, but he was afraid I might still be ignorant of what a miserable condition I had plunged myself into through my curiosity. Hereupon the good man was pronounced free, and I with a sad heart had to step aside.

After me the rest were called for too, and came jocundly out again, which pained me still more, for I imagined nothing other than that I must finish my life under the gate. I also had many pensive thoughts running up and down in my head, what I should do, and how to spend the time. At length I considered that I was now old, and according to the course of nature, had few years more to live. And that this anguished and melancholy life would quickly send me from this world, and then my door-keeping would be at an end, and by a most happy sleep I might quickly bring myself to the grave. I had many of these thoughts. Sometimes it vexed me that I had seen such gallant things, and must be robbed of them.

Sometimes I rejoiced that still, before my end, I had been accepted to all joy, and should not be forced to depart shamefully. This was the last and worst shock that I sustained.

During my cogitations the rest had got ready. So, after they had received a good night from the King and lords, each one was conducted into his lodging. But I, most wretched man, had nobody to show me the way, and must moreover suffer myself to be tormented; and so that I might be certain of my future function, I had to put on the ring which the other had worn before. Finally, the King exhorted me that since this was now the last time I was likely to see him in this manner, I should behave myself according to my place, and not against the order. Upon which he took me in his arms, and kissed me, all which I understood to mean that in the morning I must sit at my gate. Now after they had all spoken friendlily to me for a while, and at last given their hands, committing me to the Divine protection, I was conducted by both the old men, the Lord of the Tower, and Atlas, into a glorious lodging, in which stood three beds, and each of us lay in one of them, where we spent almost two, &c.....

(Here about two leaves in quarto are missing,
and he [the author], whereas he imagined that he must,
in the morning, be a doorkeeper, returned home.)

FINI

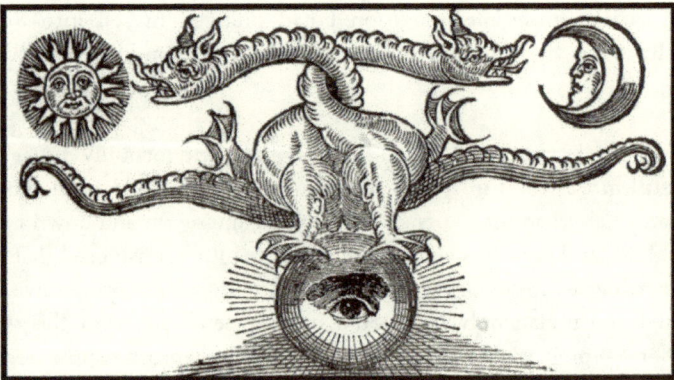

More Masonic Books from Cornerstone

Seeking Light
The Esoteric Heart of Freemasonry
by Michael R. Poll
6×9 Softcover 156 pages
ISBN: 1613422571

Measured Expectations
The Challenges of Today's Freemasonry
by Michael R. Poll
6×9 Softcover 180 pages
ISBN: 978-1613422946

Zanoni
A Rosicrucian Tale
by Edward Bulwer Lytton
6×9 Softcover 306 pages
ISBN: 161342051X

A Lodge at Labor
Freemasons and Masonry Today
by Michael R. Poll
6x9 Softcover 180 pages
ISBN 9781613423257

Alchemy
Ancient and Modern
by H. Stanley Redgrove
8.5 x 11, Softcover 160 pages
ISBN 1613420846

Cornerstone Book Publishers
www.cornerstonepublishers.com

More Masonic Books from Cornerstone

Masonic Enlightenment
The Philosophy, History and Wisdom of Freemasonry
Edited by Michael R. Poll
6 x 9 Softcover 180 pages
ISBN 1887560750

The Stone of the Philosophers
An Alchemical Handbook
Edited by Michael R. Poll
6x9 Softcover 368 pages
ISBN 1887560858

Brother of the Third Degree
by Will L. Garver
6 x 9 Softcover 228 pages
ISBN: 1887560432

Numbers
Their Occult Power And Mystic Virtues
by W. Wynn Westcott
6 x 9 Softcover 140 pages
ISBN 1934935555

The Doctrine and Literature of the Kabalah
by Arthur Edward Waite
6 x 9 Softcover 536 pages
ISBN 1613422393

Cornerstone Book Publishers
www.cornerstonepublishers.com

More Masonic Books from Cornerstone

The Initiates of the Flame
by Manly P. Hall
6 x 9 Softcover 96 pages
ISBN: 1613421990

The Canon
*An Exposition of the Pagan Mystery Perpetuated
in the Cabala as the Rule of All Arts*
by William Stirling
6 x 9 Softcover 428 pages
ISBN: 1613420854

The History of Magic
by Eliphas Levi
Translated by Arthur Edward Waite
8x10 Softcover 594 pages
ISBN 1613421559

A.E. Waite: Words From a Masonic Mystic
Edited by Michael R. Poll
Foreword by Joseph Fort Newton
6 x 9 Softcover 168 pages
ISBN: 1887560734

An Esoteric Reading of Biblical Symbolism
by Harriet Tuttle Bartlett
6 x 9 Softcover 232 pages
ISBN: 1613420803

Cornerstone Book Publishers
www.cornerstonepublishers.com

New Orleans Scottish Rite College
http://www.no-sr-college.com/

Clear, Easy to Watch
Scottish Rite / Craft Lodge
Video & Podcast Masonic Education